Blasphemy: A Very Short Introduction

VERY SHORT INTRODUCTIONS are for anyone wanting a stimulating and accessible way into a new subject. They are written by experts, and have been translated into more than 45 different languages.

The series began in 1995, and now covers a wide variety of topics in every discipline. The VSI library currently contains over 650 volumes—a Very Short Introduction to everything from Psychology and Philosophy of Science to American History and Relativity—and continues to grow in every subject area.

Very Short Introductions available now:

Available soon:

For more information visit our website

www.oup.com/vsi/

Yvonne Sherwood

BLASPHEMY

A Very Short Introduction

OXFORD
UNIVERSITY PRESS

OXFORD
UNIVERSITY PRESS

Great Clarendon Street, Oxford, OX2 6DP,
United Kingdom

Oxford University Press is a department of the University of Oxford.
It furthers the University's objective of excellence in research, scholarship,
and education by publishing worldwide. Oxford is a registered trade mark of
Oxford University Press in the UK and in certain other countries

First edition published in 2021

Impression: 1

Published in the United States of America by Oxford University Press
198 Madison Avenue, New York, NY 10016, United States of America

British Library Cataloguing in Publication Data
Data available

Library of Congress Control Number: 2021931769

ISBN 978-0-19-879757-9

Printed in Great Britain by
Ashford Colour Press Ltd, Gosport, Hampshire

Contents

Contents

List of illustrations

Chapter 1
Introduction: 'blasphemous' crucifixions

For a very long time now, people have been talking about the death of God. For an equally long time, they have been proclaiming the end of blasphemy. In a world where not everyone believes in God, 'blasphemy' is surely a concept that has passed its use-by date. And yet blasphemy (like God or religion) seems strangely resilient. It may even be on the rise. Hardly a month goes by when blasphemy is not in the news. It makes the headlines in the latest atrocities explicitly linked to blasphemy, such as the *Charlie Hebdo* massacres of 2015, or news of the latest country to repeal blasphemy laws. (And who knew that there were still blasphemy laws in, say, Iceland, or Denmark, until we heard that they were being abolished on the news?)

We could be forgiven for feeling a little confused. Is blasphemy getting its last obituary? Are we putting the final nails in blasphemy's coffin? Is this *Very Short Introduction* soon going to look like a *Very Short Introduction to the Dodo* or *Victorian Manners*—the least relevant book in the whole series? Or is blasphemy insurgent, resurgent, on the rise? And how did the crime of blasphemy, widely understood as an offence against God or the gods, pass from church (or canon) law into secular law and then stay put for over half a millennium?

These are the kinds of questions to tackle as we go on a quest to track the often surprising history of this incendiary idea.

Defining blasphemy

What *on earth* is blasphemy? How can a concept that has been associated with hurting gods have meaning down here, on earth? Though no one seems to comment on this very important point, the etymology of blasphemy comes surprisingly close to the recent idea of *hate speech*. Blasphemy means 'speech that hurts' or 'hurt to fame/reputation': to slander, defame, or deface. The first part of the word is widely understood to come from *blaptō* ('to hurt'). The second half, *phēmē*, means 'speech, talk, utterance' but also 'fame and reputation'. (Compare Latin *fama*, and the Greek goddess of rumour and reputation *Phēmē*.) Like so many words, *blasphemy* (βλασφημία/*blasphēmía*) was imported into European languages via Greek and Latin. It is a term that Christianity exported to the world. The opposite of blasphemy is *euphemism* from *euphēmein* , originally meaning 'to avoid bad words in religious rites', and now meaning 'speaking well' by avoiding words that are too embarrassing or harsh.

According to these not very precise definitions, blasphemy is speech that hurts or offends, as opposed to speech that does not. The concept also seems to have a strong social dimension: damage to the reputation or face. The dictionaries also agree that blasphemy is somehow religious, defining blasphemy as 'profane speaking' or 'speaking sacrilegiously' about 'God or sacred things'. The repetition of words like *sacrilege* ('stealing/violating sacred things') and *profanation* (a word derived from the Latin 'outside the temple [*fanum*]') reinforces a general vague sense that blasphemy is somehow about disrespecting, or being outside or against, gods and sacred spaces and holy things.

Blasphemy is a very open concept, leaving a great deal of room for manoeuvre and interpretation. What/who counts as sacred?

What/who counts as sacred enough to be protected? How offensive must a speech or act be to register as a blasphemy? Can blasphemies (and punishments) be ranked on a scale from mild to harsh, like the classification of hard and soft (class A and class B) drugs, or degrees of injury and pain? And how can a sensation of pain be *shared*? By definition, blasphemy seems to be in the ears and eyes of the receiver. This is a concept that tends to rely on the witness of those (gods or people) who feel they have been hurt/ defamed, or those who speak on their behalf. It is a concept, therefore, that is likely to get us guessing about the experiences and feelings of other people, and maybe even gods.

Blasphemous crucifixions

In an obscenity trial in the USA in 1964, the Supreme Court Justice Potter Stewart controversially announced: 'I know [obscenity] when I see it.' On a recent birthday trip to a hugely popular West End show, my son and I felt about as sure as one could possibly be that we had seen something blasphemous, meaning something that we felt that other people, as we imagined them, would/could see as blasphemous. As someone who has studied blasphemy for over ten years, I was particularly impressed with how energetically the musical ticked all the boxes. There was a particularly enthusiastic performance of cursing God; an extremely irreverent take on that common 'blasphemous' practice of mixing holy figures and animals (in this case, a frog); and plenty of unorthodox sex. But this musical has not, in fact, been tagged with *#blasphemy*, and happily plays in the West End, while Richard Thomas and Stewart Lee's *Jerry Springer: The Opera* was consigned to relative oblivion by Christian protesters.

So what makes a blasphemy? It might help to look at some key ideas using the example of Jesus on the cross.

Crucifixion was a Roman device for physical and social torture. Just like blasphemy, crucifixion involved defacing the public

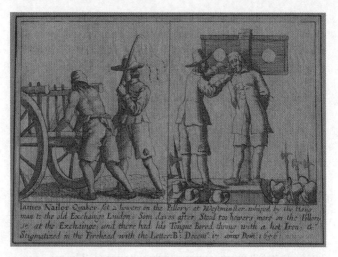

James Nailor Quaker. Set 2 howers on the Pillory at Westminster whiped by the Hang
man to the old Exchainge London: Som dayes after, Stood too howers more on the Pillory
yr at the Exchainge, and there had his Tongue Bored, throw with a hot Iron, &
Stigmatized in the Forehead with the Letter:B: Decem: 17 anno Dom: 1656

1. The public torture and humiliation of James Nayler, branded with a B on his forehead and almost executed for blasphemy in 1656.

persona, turning him (and occasionally her) into a grotesque living caricature. As Seneca observes, bodies were crucified in a range of humiliating positions: upside down, or with the arms 'stretched out...on a forked gibbet', or with the genitals impaled. To mock his lofty social status, one victim was crucified on a big white cross. Jesus's messianic claims were brutally parodied in the crown of thorns and the notice 'The King of the Jews'.

Figure 1 shows the ritual humiliation of the Quaker James Nayler, convicted of blasphemous actions 'derogatory to the honour of God, and destructive to humane Society' for imitating the passion of Christ by riding into Bristol with his followers on a donkey on Palm Sunday, 1656. Having narrowly escaped execution (eighty-two voted for execution, and ninety-six against), Nayler was whipped through the streets, then forced to stand in the pillory, which looked very like a cross. His forehead was 'stigmatized' or branded with a letter B for blasphemer and his tongue was bored through with a hot iron. Quaker accounts lament the 'crucifixion' of their

2. Stone rubbing of Greek graffito from Rome, c.200 CE. The caption reads: 'Alexamenos worships god' or 'Alexamenos, worship God!'.

leader. Nayler put a piece of paper on his own forehead: 'It is written (Luke 23.38) "This is the King of the Jews"'.

So what counts and has counted as a blasphemous crucifixion or a blasphemous imitation of Christ? Riding into Bristol on a donkey? What about presenting a Christian worshipping a donkey? Or a frog or a monkey on a cross?

The graffito in Figure 2—found on a wall in Rome—certainly looks pretty blasphemous. It takes the social humiliation of the crucifixion and repeats it, in the form of an improvised cartoon.

Today the crucifixion is the widely recognized logo or sign of Christianity. But until the 6th century it was never used by Christians—only by those who wanted to mock Christianity. This drawing, known as the Alexamenos graffito, conflates two popular Roman caricatures of Christianity (popular, that is, among the few who noticed the new religion) as, in the words of rhetorician Marcus Cornelius Fronto, a 'foolish' religion, based on the 'worship [of] a *crucified* man' and the 'worship [of] the head of an ass'.

Alexamenos may well have been extremely hurt by this portrayal of his saviour as a crucified donkey. But because the graffito dates from a time when Christianity was, in (anachronistic) modern terms, a minority religion, he could never have launched any protest about 'blasphemy'. Blasphemy needs a social and legal context; and blasphemy tends to be about protecting the religion of the majority. Content alone is not enough.

In contrast, a crucified frog by the German artist Martin Kippenberger with the title *Feet First* became blasphemous in 2008, twenty-eight years after it was first made in 1990, and nine years after the artist's death. The work became 'blasphemous' when the leader of the regional government, Franz Pahl, went on hunger strike to protest the inclusion of the offensive amphibian in an exhibition at the Museion art museum in Bolzano, Italy. By going on hunger strike, Pahl dramatically performed, on his own body, the concept of *religious hurt*: a sensation of inner pain that cannot easily be shared. By deliberately starving his body, he was trying to represent (he said) the 'wounds' that the frog inflicted on 'the religious sentiments of so many people who see in the cross the symbol of God's love'. Verdicts of blasphemy are not just passed by gods (or those who speak for gods), and judges and juries. They can also be passed by a film classification board or a museum management committee, or a politician or members of the public.

Unlike Kippenberger's frog, an ape on the cross by artist Paul Fryer does not come up in a Google search for blasphemies. If you google *The Privilege of Dominion* (2009) you find it, instead, rather surprisingly, in *The Church Times*. Did the crucified waxwork gorilla pass under the blasphemy radar because the artist's stated aim was to 'highlight the plight of the Western Lowland Gorillas'? But how did this clear expression of the maker's intention get the work off the hook, given that the concept of blasphemy emphasizes the experience of the beholder, and is relatively indifferent to the maker's intention? Or did the crucified monkey not qualify as blasphemy because no one noticed, or went on hunger strike to protest? In 2007, Fryer exhibited a brutal modern crucifixion called *Pietà (The Empire never Ends)*—a bruised waxwork Christ being executed in an electric chair—at the Cathédrale Notre-Dame-et-Saint-Arnoux de Gap in the French Alps. In an interview with *Le Monde*, Monsignor Jean-Michel de Falco *praised* Fryer for resurrecting the 'scandal' of the cross and for attracting 'a large number of people who don't set foot in a church'. Seeming 'blasphemies' can be celebrated and commissioned by religious communities. We will discuss the phenomenon of *inner-religious blasphemy* in more detail in Chapter 3.

Blasphemy is a litmus test of changing values: a marker of how the limits of the thinkable, the sayable, and the presentable change over time. This is particularly obvious in the case of gender and sex.

A contemporary visitor to the Museum of the Diocese Graz-Sackau in Austria might be shocked to find a statue of a woman, with skirts and a beard, hanging on the cross, looking for all the world like a trans-Christ, or Christ-as-Conchita-Wurst. But in fact s/he is an 18th-century sculpture of the entirely traditional figure of St Wilgefortis. A gallery visitor looking at Maarten van Heemskerck's *Man of Sorrows* of 1532, or Peter Paul Rubens's *Resurrected Christ Triumphant* (*c.*1616) might be taken aback to see Jesus with a visible erection. But in fact the artists were aiming for biological literalism (the penis of a dying man does

7

stiffen, apparently) and a symbolic assertion of physical resurrection—life triumphant!

Modern viewers are *more* likely to see these crucifixions as potentially 'blasphemous' because we live on the other side of the sexual revolutions and equal rights movements of the 1960s, which have led to new and tense public conflicts between religion and gender/sex. Since the artist Edwina Sandys made the first bare-breasted woman on the cross, known as *Christa*, in 1984, women on the cross—like black Jesuses—have become figures of activist salvation to some, and blasphemy to others. When Christa was first placed in the Manhattan Cathedral Church of St John the Divine in 1984, the Dean of the Cathedral celebrated her but the Bishop of New York ordered that this 'blasphemous' woman be banished from sacred space.

Campaigns for gay rights have led to new 'blasphemies' that would have been unthinkable before the late 1960s: gay Jesuses, and Jesuses who actively enjoy sex. Early examples include Dutch author Gerhard Corneilius van het Reve's book *Nearer to Thee* (1966); the Danish artist and director Jens Jørgen Thorsen's failed attempts in the early 1970s to make a film called *The Sex Life of Jesus*—one of the many 'blasphemies' that were never made; and, most famously, James Kirkup's poem 'The Love that Dares to Speak its Name', published in *Gay News* in 1976 and successfully prosecuted in 1977. Kirkup's poem—which presents the centurion at the foot of the cross recalling Jesus's sex life and penetrating Jesus's still warm corpse—earned the editor of *Gay News* a fine and a suspended prison sentence.

Without relating the concept to blasphemy, philosopher Charles Taylor introduces the useful concept of *hypergoods*, meaning ultimate values, values that are prized above all others. Blasphemies seem to have particular traction and cultural power when they stage a conflict between hypergoods that are deeply felt, on both sides—and clearly defined. LGBTI rights campaigners have used gay Jesuses to campaign for the hypergoods of LGBTI rights and sexual freedom. Many Christians have defined themselves in contrast as defenders of the hypergood of 'family values'. Blasphemies become blasphemies when they present key conflicts in a pithy and provocative way. Gay Jesuses—and sexualized representations of other famous religious figures—have become one of the most common blasphemy memes post-1960s, because audiences recognize the new flashpoint between religion and campaigns for sexual freedom and LGBTI rights.

Not all 'blasphemies', however, involve weighty battles over hypergoods. Many blasphemous crucifixions have been accidental. In 2011, over 100 Lebanese Christians gathered in front of the Big Sale bargain clothing store in Beirut to force the owner, a Shi'a Muslim, to remove a blasphemous flip-flop. The flip-flop design appears to be a Halloween print: a graveyard, flying bats, and tombs—but also a tombstone cross—meaning that any wearer will (inadvertently) put the holy sign of the cross under his/her feet. This accidentally blasphemous 'crucifixion' was like the expensive blasphemy mass-produced by Nike, when the word *Air*, in Arabic, on the sole and uppers of the new Air shoe, was designed in such a way that it looked very like the Arabic calligraphy for the word 'Allah'. Nike issued a public apology and around 38,000 shoes were recalled.

Blasphemy is time-sensitive—and also sensitive to context, and what literature professor David Lawton helpfully calls the 'social ecology' of a particular time and place. Times, tones, and public aesthetics change, and so do blasphemies. Even the most outrageous and daring 19th-century blasphemer would never have thought, for a moment, of using a homosexual Jesus in his freedom-from-religion campaign.

Old blasphemies can pass their 'shock-by date' and start to look tame. Something that did not show up on the 'blasphemy' radar in the past can suddenly trigger new forms of social pain. When we watched *Monty Python's Life of Brian* (1979) forty years later, in 2019, the students in my blasphemy class were most scandalized by the use of blackface (which did not even get a mention in an edited collection on the film published in 2015). The class was also unanimous that the real scandal of Kirkup's 'The Love that Dares to Speak its Name' was necrophilia: the rape of a dead body. It was hard for us to understand, looking back across the decades, why many supporters and protesters in the 1970s spoke as if this poem was simply about 'being gay'. We concluded that the strange conflation of being gay with raping a dead body told us a great deal about the massive stigma attached, in the 1970s, to coming out as gay.

Dictionary definitions of blasphemy as 'speaking sacrilegiously' about 'God or sacred things' suggest that blasphemy is somehow a purely religious crime. But this seems inaccurate, as many prosecuted crucifixions have targeted politics, nationalism, and complicity between religion and the state. Examples include *Christ with Gas Mask* by the Berlin Dada artist George Grosz, from the series *Hintergrund* (Background) (1928), and Pier Paolo Pasolini's short 1962 film *La Ricotta*, named after the cheese. (Ideally I would have exhibited Georg Groz's *Christ with Gas Mask* here, but the image had to be deleted, not for reasons of 'blasphemy', as in the 1930s, but for the far more pedestrian reason of copyright fees.)

The caption to Grosz's *Christ with Gas Mask* reads 'Maul halten under weiter dienen/Shut up and do your duty'. Other lithographs in the series include a preacher spewing bullets and grenades from the pulpit, and a phonograph and saluting ink-pen being paid by a giant hand dishing out coins to trumpet 'Hurras' for war. Grosz, who Anglicized his first name and Slavicized his surname as a protest against German nationalism, was prosecuted for blasphemy, fined, then exonerated, then the exoneration was annulled—but no final judgment was reached because in 1933 he fled to the United States.

Grosz's work was later paraded by the National Socialists in the exhibition *Entartete 'Kunst'* (Degenerate 'Art'): the famous anti-exhibition or hall of shame for artworks deemed to have 'insult[ed] German feeling'. Pier Paolo Pasolini was also prosecuted for hurting national/religious feelings, or in the words of Italian law 'insulting *the religion of the state*' (my emphasis). In 1963, Pasolini was convicted and sentenced to four months in prison—a sentence that was overturned on appeal after a three year legal ordeal. *La Ricotta* is a powerful satire on religion, colonialism, racism, decadence, and indifference to poverty. As a group of actors re-enact a tableau vivant of the *Deposition from the Cross* by Jacopo Pontormo (1523–5), black actors intrude into the death of this very white Jesus, and the high dignity of the sacred scene is subverted by the jaunty soundtrack of Carolo Rustichelli's 'Ricotta Twist'. A poor extra, Stracci (meaning 'Rags'), who plays the thief on the cross, accidentally starves to death on the set—but only after telling the unsympathetic actor playing Jesus that he is so hungry that he could blaspheme.

It is always important, as we have done here, to observe how blasphemy operates *in practice*. Blasphemy is never purely about content. It needs a social and legal context, and tends to favour the values of the majority. Contra the dictionary definitions which suggest that blasphemy is a purely religious crime, many blasphemies seem to have registered as 'blasphemies' because they targeted the nation and the complicity between church and state. Blasphemy is a concept that is, by definition, in the eyes and ears of the receiver. But if some seeming-'blasphemies' are *celebrated* and commissioned by religious communities, then trying to guess what might hurt religious communities might be a tricky business, to say the least.

Chapter 2
Blasphemy in scarequotes

Blasphemy is a different kind of topic to others in the *Very Short Introduction* series. It is not like Hobbes, biometrics, migration, or electricity: people, technologies, and phenomena that clearly exist. But nor is it quite like, say, the 'Renaissance': a word that is sometimes put in quotation marks to show that this idea of an epoch was constructed by later generations. Quotation marks around 'the Renaissance' show that the concept should be taken with a pinch of salt. They do not mean that we should ban the Renaissance, or that it is a meaningless or dangerous idea. 'Blasphemy', in contrast, often appears in harsher quotation marks: the ones called scarequotes, shudder quotes, or even sneer quotes. Blasphemy is particularly interesting because it has always been accompanied by a health warning and the argument that blasphemy does not and should not exist.

Naboth's vineyard

Here's an old story, a once-upon-a-time. (As the narrator of the 'blasphemous' novel *The Satanic Verses* puts it: 'It was and it was not so, as the old stories used to say, it happened and it never did.') Once upon a time, there was a man called Naboth whose family had owned a vineyard for generations. He was fortunate. The area had gentrified and turned into the equivalent of Kensington or Mayfair. The family land was now a piece of prime real estate, right next to the palace of the king. The king looked enviously over the fence at Naboth's land. He wanted to annex it for a nice little vegetable garden. But Naboth resisted, using the traditional form of the vow, swearing on the name of God: 'The Lord forbid that I should give you my ancestral inheritance.' Like an ancient Woody Guthrie, he declared, 'This land is my land. Our land. *God forbid*.'

But the poor king really wanted his vegetable patch. He sulked. He went to bed, hid his face, and refused to eat.

Luckily the king was married to a resourceful if rather dominant queen. She taunted him for his weakness. 'Isn't sovereignty all about command of territory? What does it mean to be king if you can't even get a little tiny piece of land? Do you rule? Are you a *man*? Are you a *king*?' The queen took matters into her own hands. She reassured her husband: 'Get up and eat. I will give you Naboth's vineyard.' She then wrote letters in the king's name, sealed with his seal, addressed to all the nobles who lived in Naboth's city:

> Proclaim a fast, and seat Naboth at the head of the assembly; seat two scoundrels opposite him, and have them bring a charge against him, saying 'You have cursed/blasphemed God and the king'. Then take him out and stone him to death.

The nobles and the scoundrels did exactly as they had been told. Naboth was falsely accused, stoned to death, and the king got his vegetable patch. So everyone (that is, everyone who was still alive) lived happily ever after.

But of course, the narrator does not expect that intelligent readers will live happily or comfortably with this picture of the king growing turnips over Naboth's dead body.

This is, in fact, a long-forgotten Bible story, over two and a half millennia old: the story of Naboth's vineyard in 1 Kings 21. This is not one of the famous Bible memes that survived the fading of biblical literacy (like the nativity, the crucifixion, or the garden of Eden), though you may well recognize the name of Jezebel, the story's notorious bad queen. In introductions to blasphemy, the Old Testament/Hebrew Bible is usually represented by *legal* texts, particularly Exodus 22:28, 'You shall not blaspheme God or curse a leader of your people', and Leviticus 24, where a man who accidentally blasphemes during a fight is taken outside the camp and stoned to death. These examples are repeated over and over again because they are simple, easy to understand, and fit with common expectations of the religious past. Gods and kings support each other and demand respect. The lesson seems to be pretty straightforward, and enforced by the death penalty: 'Thou Shalt Not Blaspheme!'

Blasphemy becomes more complicated when we think about the Bible as *ta biblia*, meaning 'the library' in Greek, and consider the more ambiguous *narrative* traditions. Biblical traditions are multivalent, and often in dialogue, or conflict. In Exodus 22:28 kings and gods join forces as a united front of authority. In the Naboth story, God sends his prophet Elijah to judge the monarchs and give them the blood-curdling oracle: 'Thus says the Lord: In the place where dogs licked up the blood of Naboth, dogs will also lick up your blood.'

If it feels surprising to find a story that is so sceptical about blasphemy in (of all places) the Bible, we might have to rethink our ideas of religion. The old religious story comes strangely close to the secular modern attack on 'blasphemy' that we will look at later in this chapter. The lesson seems to be: 'Beware "blasphemy", since blasphemy charges can be fake, a mask for realpolitik.' Blasphemy is about defamation, de-facing, hurting the reputation—as we saw in Chapter 1—and this story can also be read as a social blasphemy against the king and queen. Defacing kings has often been a very dangerous business. In 1831 Charles Philipon was fined, imprisoned, and sent to an institution for the mentally ill for the crime of 'contempt of the king's person', for having drawn hilarious cartoons of King Louis Philippe of France as a pear-head in his newspaper *La Caricature* (see Figure 3).

Similarly, the story of Naboth's vineyard presents the king as a vegetable head—but in a verbal cartoon. The king is petulant, narcissistic—and therefore extremely dangerous. His queen uses trumped-up 'blasphemy' charges to obtain land—but not vital land, just a little vegetable patch. The readers and hearers of the story, most of whom have no political power, are invited to enjoy the temporary literary power that comes from mocking authority with darkly pleasurable word-caricatures.

Contemporary Naboths: blasphemy as a screen for realpolitik

The Naboth story can be read as a dark religious commentary on the many contemporary blasphemy cases where 'blasphemy' is *blasphemy in scarequotes*: a smokescreen for realpolitik.

There are numerous contenders for contemporary Naboths. One candidate would be the Chinese Christian Indonesian politician Basuki Tjahaja Purnama, commonly known as BTP or Ahok, who was sentenced to twenty months' imprisonment for blasphemy at a very convenient time for his political opponents, during his campaign for re-election as governor of Jakarta in 2017. Blasphemy charges were based on strategically edited footage of a political speech, which altered BTP's outspoken words about his opponents' *misuse* of the Qur'an to make it seem as if he had been criticizing the Qur'an itself.

Since BTP had considerable political power, he is a less appropriate match for Naboth than Mashal Khan, a journalism student at Abdul Wali Khan University in Pakistan, who was brutally attacked and killed by a lynch mob of at least sixty-one university staff and students in the

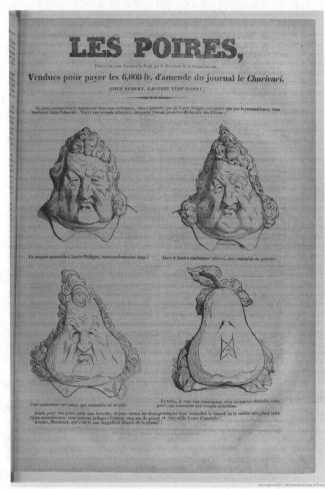

3. Blaspheming the king: the face of King Louis-Philippe goes pear-shaped in the periodical *La Caricature*, 1831.

same year, 2017. The vigilante attack on Mashal Khan was incited by a fake letter—like Jezebel's letter to the rogues instructing them to bring false charges. The letter, pinned to the university noticeboard, announced that, following the Prime Minister Nawaz Sharif's crackdown on blasphemous material on social media, an Inquiry Committee had been set up to probe into Khan's 'blasphemous activities'. The fake letter from the authorities was later withdrawn and Mashal Khan was posthumously vindicated. He had done nothing more than criticize the university for corruption, exorbitant fees, and no guarantee of students receiving their degrees. The walls of his student hostel room were plastered with statements of praise for Allah and Muhammad and quotes from Che Guevara and Marx.

Ashraf Fayadh, an artist and poet born in Gaza, was arrested after a complaint to the Saudi Committee for the Prohibition of Vice and Promotion of Virtue, a complaint that his lawyer argued originated in personal conflict with another Saudi citizen. He was convicted on the basis of conversations in a coffee shop in Abha, Twitter posts, images on his mobile phone, and poems in his collection, *Instructions Within*. The collection, available in English translation, includes poems with titles such as 'On the virtues of oil over blood', 'The name of a masculine dream', 'Equal opportunities', 'Prayers of longing', and 'The severe syndrome of home'. They confront issues such as sexual discrimination, the sacrifice of life to oil, and the suffering of Palestinian refugees. Ashraf Fayadh was sentenced to death, then to an eight-year prison term with 800 lashes, in 2015—the same year that the Saudi Arabian ambassador joined the world leaders marching in Paris, denouncing the *Charlie Hebdo* murders as 'a cowardly terrorist act'; and also the same year that the blogger Raif Badawi was given a public flogging for 'insulting Islam'. Fayadh's sentence was changed (again) to a death sentence in 2017—the same year that he received the Oxfam/Pen International award for freedom of expression.

A spokesperson for Human Rights Watch described Fayadh's offence as a perceived violation of 'government-mandated views' on 'religion, society and politics'. This description could also be applied to the far more widely publicized case of Pussy Riot, which received global coverage and support from a wide range of public figures from the Red Hot Chili Peppers to Madonna and Hillary Clinton. Three members of the band (Maria Alyokhina, Nadezhda Tolokonnikova, and Yekaterina Samutsevich) were subjected to a public show trial and sentenced to two years' imprisonment in a penal colony, following the famous one minute and thirty-four second flash gig (still available on YouTube) at the Christ the Saviour Cathedral, Moscow, on 21 February 2012 (see Figure 4).

This was an attack on religion, society and politics, as this extract from the lyrics makes very clear:

Virgin mother of God, drive away Putin!
Drive away Putin, drive away Putin!
Black frock, golden epaulettes
Parishioners crawl bowing [toward the priest, during the Eucharist]
Freedom's ghost [has gone to] heaven
A gay-pride parade [has been] sent to Siberia in shackles
Their chief saint is the head of the KGB
He leads a convoy of protesters to jail
So as not to insult the Holiest One
Woman should bear children and love
Shit, shit, the Lord's shit! (or Crap, crap, this godliness crap!)
Shit, shit, the Lord's shit!
Virgin birth-giver of God, become a feminist!
Become a feminist, become a feminist!

The punk prayer was performed just after mass protests against fraudulent parliamentary elections and the appointment of Patriarch Kirill Gundayev, a former KGB officer, as head of the Russian Orthodox Church. The line about the 'chief saint' from the KGB refers to Gundayev, who had just praised Vladimir

4. Pussy Riot's 'blasphemous' performance at the Christ the Saviour Cathedral, Moscow, 21 February 2012.

Putin, incredibly, as a 'miracle from God'. As well as protesting the collusion between the Russian Orthodox Church and the Kremlin, the punk prayer attacked incendiary new legislation, including restrictions on public protests, a new law forbidding LGBTI 'propaganda', and the introduction of compulsory 'religious enlightenment' classes in secular schools. By charging Pussy Riot with 'hooliganism incited by *religious* hatred' and '*pure…malicious blasphemy (koshchunstvo)*' (my emphases), the Russian state strategically used blasphemy to repress *political* protest. Disproportionate attention to the band members' sexuality and an exclusive focus on crimes such as 'offending religious sensibilities' and 'hurting the feelings of religious believers' effectively distracted from the major political issues at stake.

Perhaps the closest case to the biblical example of Naboth is the case of Asia Bibi, or Aasiya Noreen ('Bibi' is simply the epithet for a mature woman), the mother of five who spent eight years in solitary confinement in a prison in Lahore, as the first woman to be sentenced to death for blasphemy, before her acquittal on the grounds of insufficient evidence by the Supreme Court of Pakistan in October 2018. Aasiya was an itinerant worker in the small village of Ittanwala (simply meaning 'village number three') in the Punjab. She was a lower-caste Christian woman and the only Christian woman in the village. In her biography, she compares being a member of a religious minority to 'being an orphan in your own country'. The 'blasphemy' accusation against Aasiya Noreen came down to nothing more than a conflict over falsa berries, a water-pump, and a goat—just like Naboth's death over a vegetable patch and a piece of land (see Figure 5).

According to Aasiya's story, as dictated to the French journalist, Anne-Isabelle Tollet, 'blasphemy' charges spiralled from an everyday local conflict between Aasiya and her long-time local nemesis Musarat, who were already at odds over Aasiya's goat

5. Naboth's vineyard 2010: the water pump in Ittanwala ('village number three'), Punjab at the centre of the Asia Bibi blasphemy controversy.

having broken Musarat's water trough. Aasiya was asked to fetch water from the well by her Muslim co-workers, but was then accused of dipping her own cup and making the water undrinkable, *haram*. Musarat and the other women rounded on Aasiya, called Jesus a 'bastard', and goaded her to convert and save herself from her 'filthy religion'. Aasiya retorted by saying that Jesus was superior to Muhammad; Jesus had saved mankind; and it was her Muslim neighbours who should convert.

News of Aasiya's blasphemies was amplified by the loudspeakers of the local mosque—simultaneously spreading the news of the blasphemies and salaciously adding to the content. During Noreen's imprisonment, her defender and the outspoken opponent of the blasphemy law, Salman Taseer, governor of Punjab, was assassinated by his bodyguard Mumtaz Qadri. Qadri was sentenced to death and his body now lies in a popular shrine on the outskirts of Islamabad, adorned with rose petals. Shahbaz

Bhatti, the Christian leader of the Pakistan People's Party, was also assassinated for having publicly defended Aasiya and for calling for reforms to the blasphemy laws. When acquitted, Aasiya Noreen could not leave the prison because the single-issue anti-blasphemy party, the TLP (Tehreek-e-Labbaik Pakistan), was staging mass public protests and calling for her execution. Aasiya was finally granted asylum in Canada after having been refused unconditional asylum by both the Vatican and the then Prime Minister Theresa May in the UK. In their landmark decision on 31 October 2018, the Pakistan Supreme Court declared, in a court judgment that sounds rather like prophet Elijah's judgment on Queen Jezebel and King Ahab:

> It is ironic that in the Arabic language the appellant's name Asia means 'sinful', since in the circumstances of the present case she appears to be a person, in the words of Shakespeare's King Lear, 'more sinned against than sinning'.

Jesus and Socrates

Jesus and Socrates have somewhat greater celebrity status than Naboth, as the founding fathers of Christianity and philosophy respectively. There are no famous paintings of the death of Naboth, but the deaths of Socrates and Jesus are all over the walls of art galleries and cathedrals. It is often claimed that Europe and the so-called 'West' are founded on the twin pillars of Christianity and classical antiquity. What is often forgotten is the fact that the founding figures of Christianity and philosophy were both tried for 'blasphemy' (in inverted commas) and sentenced to death.

Socrates (c.470–399 BCE) carried out his own execution by drinking hemlock after being tried and convicted by the court of Athens for *asebeia* ('impiety'). Specifically, Socrates was condemned for being a *neologian*—a poet or maker of new gods. He was brought to trial for 'inventing new gods and denying the existence of old ones' and corrupting the youth.

The *Euthyphro*, a philosophical dialogue set just before his trial, is a very good example of the kind of philosophical and theological mischief that Socrates regularly got up to—and the reasons for it. Socrates' sparring partner, Euthyphro, is so convinced that he knows what is good and holy that he is prepared to commit the ultimate social blasphemy and execute his own father, who seems to have been caught up in an unfortunate chain of accidents. One of Euthyphro's father's servants accidentally killed another in a drunken brawl; then, while Euthyphro's father was away piously seeking direction from the gods about what kind of punishment the culprit deserved, the murderer died. In zealous Euthyphro's not very fine-tuned view, this makes his father a murderer. No ifs, no buts. He must be executed, because morality and the gods demand it—and because the gods set an example of punishing their own fathers. As Euthyphro eagerly explains, he is justified in taking action against his own father because the divine Cronos was punished by his son Zeus.

Socrates makes a number of points in this dialogue that are relevant to the discussion of blasphemy. True holiness is not expressed by persecuting and even executing offenders (like Euthyphro's father, or Socrates himself, awaiting trial). How can we be absolutely certain about the holy, or what the gods do and do not like—especially given conflicting traditions where the gods fight with one another and seem to express different views? Slavishly following the example of the gods of myth—the kinds of gods who seem to have bodies and voices—is *dangerous*. 'Do you really believe the gods fought with one another, and had dire quarrels, battles and the like, as the poets say…Are all these tales of the gods true?' Socrates asks. As ever, Socrates bests his opponent in the argument. Plato's dialogue is constructed so as to make the reader feel that Socrates' *asebeia* ('impiety') is absolutely necessary. Mocking the old gods and striving for new and safer ideas of god/the holy seems to be an important public and philosophical service, as long as pious zealots like Euthyphro are happy to execute their own fathers in faithful obedience to the gods of myth.

According to the account of Jesus's death as told in the gospels of Mark and Matthew, Jesus was accused and tried for blasphemy (like Socrates, but unlike Naboth, who was never dignified with a trial):

> Now the chief priests and the whole council were looking for testimony against Jesus to put him to death; but they found none. For many gave false testimony against him, and their testimony did not agree. Some stood up and gave false testimony against him, saying, 'We heard him say, "I will destroy this temple that is made with hands, and in three days I will build another, not made with hands."' But even on this point their testimony did not agree. Then the high priest stood up before them and asked Jesus, 'Have you no answer? What is it that they testify against you?' But he was silent and did not answer. Again the high priest asked him, 'Are you the Messiah, the Son of the Blessed One?' Jesus said, 'I am; and you will see the Son of Man seated at the right hand of the Power, and coming with the clouds of heaven.'
>
> Then the high priest tore his clothes and said, 'Why do we still need witnesses? You have heard his blasphemy! What is your decision?' All of them condemned him as deserving death. Some began to spit on him, to blindfold him, and to strike him, saying to him, 'Prophesy!' The guards also took him over and beat him.

(Mark 14:53–65; cf. Matthew 26)

The gospel narrative seems deliberately unclear. Are the witnesses false witnesses, as in the case of Naboth? Or has Jesus actually uttered statements that his accusers regard as 'blasphemous', but that he and his followers regard as truth? Either way, 'blasphemy' is a contested category in inverted commas. Either blasphemy is in the eyes or ears of the beholder or hearer (one person's truth is another person's blasphemy), or it is a trumped-up charge. After resolutely staying silent, Jesus finally utters a statement about being the messiah. The high priest clearly regards this as 'blasphemous'. But the readers of the New Testament are intended to regard this as truth, a truth all the more true for being shocking, 'blasphemous': Jesus is indeed the messiah.

Even as the Gospel makes the 'blasphemous' declaration that Jesus is the messiah, it also presents Jesus as deliberately *avoiding* blasphemy by refusing to mention the name of God. Rather than naming God directly, he refers euphemistically to 'the Power'.

The stories of Jesus and Socrates are told in such a way that our sympathies are with the 'blasphemers' and *against* the ones who accuse them. We have an English noun for the blasphemers, but no equivalent word for the 'ones-who-are-(extremely)-sensitive-to-blasphemy', or the 'ones-who-bring-a-charge-of-blasphemy'. This is unfortunate, because their role is very important, perhaps even more important than the 'blasphemers'. We should invent a noun for them so that this important function is not missed. There is no stereotype of the ones-who-are-enraged-by-blasphemy in Plato's account of the trial and death of Socrates. The men of Athens respect Socrates' status as a fellow citizen and put execution to the vote. The New Testament starts the tradition of depicting the accusers as verbal caricatures. The Jewish high priest in the Gospel account of Jesus's trial cannot bear blasphemy. He has a profound blasphemy allergy. He tears his clothes in horror, crying for blood. Others spit on Jesus and externalize the pain that they ostensibly feel by inflicting real wounds on Jesus's body.

The Gospel writer clearly intends for us to sympathize with the victim and condemn those who are so sensitive to blasphemy that they react by torturing and killing the offender. He exaggerates these caricatures to get his point across. Thomas Woolston (1668–1733)—a convicted 'blasphemer' who died in prison—realised that the 'base and unnatural resentment' and excessive 'indignation' ascribed to the Jews in the New Testament was so outrageous that it was obviously an exaggeration. Many readers have been less perceptive than Woolston, and have continued to read the caricature as literal truth. You can see the enduring power of this snarling, blasphemy-phobic caricature if you look at recent films such as Mel Gibson's *The Passion of the Christ*, or the stoning scene in *Monty Python's Life of Brian*.

The biblical caricature is even more cartoonish in the story of the stoning of the apostle Stephen in the book of Acts, which is like a mixture of Jesus's trial and the trumped up charge against Naboth (Acts 6:8–7:60). Having failed to best the apostle in argument, the Jews 'secretly instigate' false witnesses to say, 'We have heard [Stephen] speak blasphemous words against Moses and God.' When they hear Stephen's account of truth, they 'become enraged and grind their teeth', cover their ears, rush on him, and stone him in a frenzy—hardly a measured and judicial execution. The heroic martyr Stephen prays with his last breath for their forgiveness before he expires.

Parrhēsía

Unlike Naboth, who utters only one line of resistance—'The Lord forbid that I should give you my ancestral inheritance'—then sits, silently, on the land of his ancestors, Jesus and Socrates *speak*, and their words are recorded reverently by disciple-amanuenses (the Gospel writers and Socrates' student, Plato, respectively). Jesus's and Socrates' teachings can be described as *parrhesía*, a term first used in the 5th century BCE meaning 'to speak everything', 'to speak boldly'. The term is used to describe Jesus's speech and the speech of the apostles (e.g. Acts 4:13). It implies bold speech to a higher authority, not someone who is beneath you—and therefore danger and risk. As French historian of ideas Michel Foucault puts it:

> *Parrhesía* is a verbal activity in which a speaker expresses his personal relationship to truth, and risks his life because he

26

Blasphemy

recognizes truth-telling as a duty to improve or help other people (as well as himself). In *parrhēsía*, the speaker uses his freedom and chooses frankness instead of persuasion, truth instead of falsehood or silence, the risk of death instead of life and security, criticism instead of flattery, and moral duty instead of self-interest and moral apathy.

Socrates famously described himself as a 'gadfly', whose god-given task was to 'sting' the citizens of Athens. Jesus was a Galilean, who grew up just over thirty miles from the major centre (in Gadara in modern Jordan) from the group known as the Cynics—the ones who were called the 'dog-like' ones (from *kyôn*, dog), because they destroyed the conventions of human society and were known to *bite*. Like the Cynics, Jesus lived as a homeless traveller, carrying only staff and purse and cloak, and advising his followers to 'Live like the animals, like the plants, like the little children...' (Matt. 6:25–34). He didn't *quite* go so far as Diogenes the Cynic, who got his audience's attention by masturbating in public and saying 'If only it were as easy to banish hunger by rubbing my belly'! But according to some Gospel traditions, he came close. The rabble-rousing Galilean made declarations such as 'You are not sons of Abraham. You are sons of Satan', or 'You cannot follow me unless you abandon your father and mother and your family.' 'I will tear down the temple and rebuild it in three days,' he proclaimed, when he came to Jerusalem to stir the pot.

The words attributed to the two teachers are presented as an absolutely necessary shock. Socrates *must* intervene to stop gullible people like Euthyphro committing atrocities by copying the gods of myth and poetry. In the Gospels, the New Religious Movement, Christianity, is presented as coming into being through blasphemy. As George Bernard Shaw famously put it, 'All great truths begin as blasphemies.' New truth is outrageous, blasphemous. If it weren't so outrageous, so 'blasphemous', we wouldn't even recognize it as something new. It would just be a tweak on the old truths. New revelation can never simply be a polite modification of established truth.

To confirm their status as 'blasphemers', Socrates and Jesus died for their truth.

The heroic secular

On 7 January 2015, two armed brothers, Cherif and Said Kouachi, stormed into the Paris offices of the satirical French magazine *Charlie Hebdo*, shooting twelve people and injuring eleven others. Three days of horror ensued, including a prolonged siege at a Hypercacher kosher supermarket, where nineteen people were held hostage and twelve Jewish people were killed. Because witnesses testified to hearing the Kouachi brothers yell, 'We have avenged the Prophet Muhammad. We have killed Charlie Hebdo!', the atrocities were largely understood as a new battle in the old war between religion and secularization, and an unwelcome return of religious violence in the form of violent retribution for 'blasphemy'. As commentators took their cue from the Kouachi brothers, *Charlie Hebdo* and *blasphemy* were thrust into the spotlight, while other aspects of the chaos that did not fit the blasphemy paradigm received far less attention (including the Hypercacher attack).

The Place de la République at the centre of Paris became the focal point for a mass outpouring of grief and protest, which looked very like a Catholic mass. The square soon filled with candles, pencils, flags, memorials, and posters. Many of the posters clearly understood the key issue as the defence of freedom of speech against religion: a replay of the old battle between the secularizing French state and the Catholic Church. One poster proclaimed: 'Stop the war. God, religions and superstitions will pass away. The spirit (*l'esprit*) of Charlie is immortal.' The French word *l'esprit* means spirit but also wit and courage.

Shortly after the massacres, Régis Debray and Didier Leschi published a little red book with the title *Everyday Laïcité (or Everyday Secularism): A Practical Guide*, focusing on the conflict between religion and secularism. The entries included 'zeal', 'circumcision', 'caricature', 'headscarf', 'injury and blasphemy', and 'politics and faith'. The entry on 'caricature' stated:

> Satirical drawings represent…the front line of the regime of secularism (laïcité) and, in the international arena, a true line of separation between states that we could call laïque, and states that we could term clerical. Wherever political power is asserted as a spiritual power, the caricaturist is gagged.

But even this manifesto was a little divided. The entry on 'artistic freedom' argued against any legal regulation—but also added that 'a little civility' does not damage freedom, and that blasphemy should not be seen as a secular 'duty' like a 'morning prayer'.

Several careful reflections on the *Charlie Hebdo* murders have, without in any way justifying the atrocity or blaming the victims, argued that it is misleading to see making cartoons directed at religious minorities as just one more example of what the anthropologist Saba Mahmood calls the 'heroic secular': a replay of the brave old Enlightenment fight against the repressive forces of the European church. The problem lies in generalizing religion. Not all religions are equal. It makes a difference whether you are punching up at the ruling religious authorities in your own country, or mocking the sacred truths and figures of religious and ethnic minorities. Another problem with the 'secularization versus religion' framework is that it allows Western states to fudge and whitewash their own histories, and to imagine that they have always supported religious freedom, including the right to have no religious belief.

Many are shocked to discover the extent of blasphemy prosecutions in Europe—or to find out that the last man to be imprisoned for blasphemy in the UK, John William Gott, a trouser salesman from Bradford, was imprisoned for nine months with hard labour in 1921. When the *Satanic Verses* affair broke out in Bradford in 1989, no one remembered Gott, who had been imprisoned just sixty-seven years (a lifetime) earlier. This was not just an accidental memory lapse.

In Britain, the crime of blasphemy traditionally carried social penalties known as civil disabilities. We should pause for a moment to think about that phrase: *civil disabilities*. According to the 1697 Act for 'suppressing of Blasphemy and Profaneness' (William III), those educated in the Christian religion who were found guilty of blasphemy would be made 'incapable and disabled in Law to all Intents and Purposes whatsoever to have or enjoy any Office or...Imployment...Ecclesiastical Civil or Military or any Profit or Advantage appertaining to them'. They would suffer *civil disability*; be rendered incapacitated in public life. Punishment for blasphemy could only be applied to Anglican Protestants because members of other religious groups—meaning Jews, Catholics, and nonconformists (the only other religions that were visible at the time)—were already subject to civil disability. They were already 'disabled' because they were unable to pass the test for entering public office: taking holy communion according to the rites of the Church of England, and swearing allegiance to the monarch as head of the Church of England. Taking holy communion in the appropriate way allowed a man (but of course not a woman) to pass into the elite, prestigious communities of Parliament, the universities, or the law. These civil disabilities were only abolished for Catholics and nonconformists in 1828; for Jews in 1858; and for public atheists in 1888.

The idea of the 'heroic secular' might be problematic in the context of 21st-century multicultural France, but it certainly applies to blasphemy controversies of the 18th, 19th, and early 20th centuries. In Britain, Charles Bradlaugh, the first public atheist to be voted in as a Member of Parliament, was pelted with stones in the street. His friend and sparring partner, George Foote, was sent to prison for a year with hard labour for blasphemous cartoons published in his newspaper *The Freethinker* in 1882. These 'blasphemers' were activist blasphemers. They deliberately used blasphemy to make space for the new outrageous idea of the secular, and the freedom not to have any religious identity.

Coming out as a secularist or freethinker in the 19th and early 20th centuries was as risky and controversial as coming out as a 'homosexual' in the 1960s, 1970s, or 1980s. Just like campaigners for gay rights, freethinkers had to agitate to create a new visible public identity that had never existed before. The equivalents of the famous Stonewall Inn or publications like *Gay News* were the new temples and churches of secularism, like Conway Hall or the Old Street Hall of Science (nicknamed the Blasphemy Shop!) in London, and newspapers such as *The Black Dwarf*, *The Republican*, *The Freethinker*, and the *Boston Investigator*. Buildings like Conway Hall were modelled on nonconformist churches and people poured into public lectures in their thousands. Cheap newspapers like *The Freethinker* spread 'blasphemous' views at the 'people's price' of one penny.

In Chapter 1, we saw how blasphemy took a sexual, and specifically 'homosexual', turn in the late 1960s and early 1970s—so much so that one of the most common blasphemy memes is now to present Jesus and other holy figures as gay. The homosexual turn may be new, but in fact blasphemy has been in bed (so to speak) with sex for centuries. Only the limits of the thinkable—and what has counted as sexually scandalous—have changed.

There is a pretty clear photofit for convicted blasphemers in Britain and North America in the 19th and early 20th centuries. They tended to be campaigners for a package of freedoms that could not, in their view, be separated. This package of freedoms included (1) free thought (freedom from religious orthodoxy); (2) freedom of expression (freedom of the press); (3) equal political representation (universal suffrage), in many cases extending into left-leaning or anarchist politics; and often, for many (4) sexual freedom (as far as they could think it, within the limits of their own context), and particularly what we now call birth control. Blasphemy was a crime that extended, on one side, into the most intimate (the private and sexual) and, on the other side, into the public (the political). It became confused with sedition and obscenity and new 19th- and 20th-century laws on obscenity. Blasphemy was rarely purely religious (whatever that might mean). It was also about politics, and very often about sex.

John Gott, the last man to be imprisoned for blasphemy in Britain, represented the complete package, quite literally. His 'blasphemous' pamphlet *Rib-Ticklers, or Questions for Parsons* included a full-page advertisement for a big bundle of pamphlets including *Britain's Disgrace*, *An Urgent Plea for Old Age Pensions*, *Funny Bible Stories, Illustrated*, and *Sex Radicalism (Prosecuted Issue)*. The same package of issues shaped the 'blasphemous' agendas of Richard Carlile in the UK and Abner Kneeland in the USA. Richard Carlile (1790–1843), who was given the longest prison sentence for blasphemy in Britain, was imprisoned for six years under the Six Acts of 1819. The Six Acts included the Seditious Meeting Act (restrictions on public meetings of more than fifty people concerned with matters of 'church and state'); the Newspapers and Stamp Duties Act (increasing taxes on newspapers, and requiring publishers to give a financial bond for good behaviour); and the Blasphemous and Seditious Libels Act, which beefed up existing laws, increasing the maximum sentence to transportation to a penal colony for up to fourteen years. Carlile was convicted for publishing the 'blasphemous' works of the revolutionary political theorist Tom Paine in affordable pamphlets, and for using his newspapers, *The Black Dwarf* and *The Republican*, to print mock scriptures and mock liturgies. These included a fabulous parody on the British Parliament's House of Lords: 'The LORD giveth, and the LORDS taketh away. Blessed be the way of the Lords', and William Hone's *Political Litany . . . to be said or sung, until the appointed change come* (1817). Hone's mock liturgy included supplicant lines from the subject-people such as:

> O gracious, noble, right honourable, and learned rulers of our land…have mercy upon us, a poverty-stricken people

> Spare us, good Prince! From an unnational debt; from unmerited pensions and sinecure places…and from utter starvation [and] from a Parliament chosen only by one-tenth of the tax-payers

> We beseech ye to hear us, O Rulers! That it may please ye to place within the bounds of economy the expenditure of all the Royal Family…

Satire of the divine Lord blurs into mockery of the House of Lords, the political establishment, and the royal family. The worshipful language of catechisms and liturgies is used to parody the supplicant dependency into which the majority have been forced. Blasphemy often messes with tones. In papers such as *The Black Dwarf* and *The Republican*, high and holy genres were sabotaged in popular ballads and songs, just as Pasolini would later subvert the sacred scene of the crucifixion by setting it to Carolo Rustichelli's 'Ricotta Twist'.

Carlile, the man who served the longest prison sentence for blasphemy in Britain, also published the first illustration of the Peterloo Massacre in Manchester in August 1819, spreading news of the carnage that took place when drunken members of the cavalry charged into a crowd of 60,000–80,000 protesters who had gathered to demand parliamentary reform when only 2 per cent of the population had the vote. He was also the first man in Britain to write a book on birth control. While serving prison time for blasphemous libel, Carlile wrote *Every Woman's Book*, also known as *What Is Love?* Scandalously, the book promoted rudimentary contraception, sexual pleasure, and what Carlile called 'moral marriage' (monogamous marriage with the possibility of divorce if the couple fell out of love). The book attacked the repression of sexual freedom by a church that believed it 'a great merit to crucify the bodily lusts'. The first copy had a frontispiece (which was withdrawn in later editions) of Adam and Eve without their decorously positioned fig leaves (see Figure 6).

6. Adam and Eve without their neatly positioned fig leaves: frontispiece to Richard Carlile, *What Is Love?* or *Every Woman's Book* (1826).

Abner Kneeland, who was sent to prison for blasphemy for sixty days in Boston in 1834, published lectures by his British freethinking allies, including Richard Carlile and his common law (or 'moral marriage') partner, Eliza Sharples, in his newspaper the *Boston Investigator*. Communities of freethinkers joined forces across the Atlantic as print or paper friends. Abner Kneeland's 'blasphemy' was, like Carlile's, social, religious, political, and sexual—and also, in his case, racial. Kneeland was a public freethinker and a Democrat in overwhelmingly Whig Boston. As a friend of the abolitionist Francis Wright, he supported abolition *and* (very unusually) interracial marriage. In 1832, Kneeland published a second edition of *The Fruits of Philosophy, or the Private Companion of Young Married People* by his friend and fellow freethinker Dr Charles Knowlton. The euphemistically titled *Fruits of Philosophy* was a book about birth control, printed in miniature so that (not unlike the tiny vernacular Bibles of the Protestant Reformation) it could be hidden in a pocket or the palm of the hand.

The *Boston Investigator* ran an almost identical agenda to Carlile's *Republican*. The paper bore a masthead illustration of a printing press with a banner that read 'Tyrant's Foe, People's Friend' and, beneath this, under Working Man's Department, headings such as 'Universal Education', 'No Legislation on Religion', 'Equal Taxation on Property', and 'Abolition of Imprisonment for Debt'. Kneeland was convicted not so much for blasphemous content, but for spreading that blasphemous content to the masses. As the prosecution declared: 'His Journal, a Newspaper, is cheap—and sent into a thousand families. Where one man would be injured by Hume, Gibbon, or Volney, a thousand may be injured by this Newspaper so widely circulated, so easily read—so coarsely expressed—so industrially spread abroad.' After his prison sentence, a disillusioned Kneeland left Boston and moved to establish a colony of 'free inquirers' in Salubria in Iowa.

Kneeland's and Carlile's cases are only known to specialists because they do not fit with the liberal public images that the UK and the USA (especially a progressive city like Boston) like to present. Kneeland's case might seem particularly surprising. It is surprising to find a refugee from 'liberal' Boston fleeing to Iowa, now widely seen as a more religiously conservative state. Given that the First Amendment to the United States Constitution famously states that 'Congress shall make no law respecting an establishment of religion, or prohibiting the free exercise thereof; or abridging the freedom of speech, or of the press...', we might reasonably expect that 'blasphemy' has always been a dead concept in the USA. It is certainly true that 'blasphemers' have generally had a harder time in Europe, and especially Britain, than in the USA. Carlile was imprisoned for six years; Kneeland for sixty days. Kneeland was the last man to be imprisoned—but certainly not prosecuted—in the USA. Over a century after the Kneeland case, in 1952, the US Supreme Court ruled (in the case of *Joseph Burstyn, Inc. v. Wilson*) that state blasphemy laws were an unconstitutional prior restraint on freedom of speech. Yet, despite this, blasphemy laws are still on the books in six states: Michigan, Oklahoma, South Carolina, Wyoming, Pennsylvania, and Massachusetts, where Abner Kneeland was prosecuted. A prosecution for blasphemy in Pennsylvania rumbled on from 1977 to 2010.

We don't have to go back very far into US or British history to find examples of the Naboth problem: 'blasphemy' as a screen for realpolitik. Attacks on the illusion that blasphemy operates as a purely religious concept have often been at the heart of the (always unsuccessful) 19th- and 20th-century campaigns for abolishing the British blasphemy laws. In 1884, Lord Justice Sir J. F. Stephens warned that blasphemy charges 'afford a channel for the gratification of private malice under the cloak of religion'. In 1924, a deputation to the Home Secretary from the Society for the Abolition of the Blasphemy Laws pointed out that over the last two centuries blasphemy laws had been used 'as a cover for preventing political agitation...prevent[ing] copyright...prevent[ing] a parent having custody of a child...and prevent[ing] the paying over of legacies [inheritances] when it was assumed that the legacies might be used for anti-christian purposes'. 'Blasphemy' prosecutions were often an attack on 'secularism', and all the sexually and politically dangerous views that went with it. They were used to take away resources and make the social position of being a secularist/socialist untenable, unliveable. Though no one was executed in the USA or Britain in the 19th century, this policy (making a public identity taboo and unviable) is not completely different, in its logic, from the position that the states of Pakistan, Iran, or Egypt take towards ex-Muslims and undesirable 'false revelations', like the Ahmadi Muslims or the Baha'i.

Cursing parrots and the fading of belief

As a result of secularist activism, new norms of freedom of religion and freedom from religion were established, including the right to have no religious belief. In this context, the idea of blasphemy in scarequotes took on a new meaning. As the convicted 'blasphemer' George Foote put it, in a statement which is often quoted by secular societies and campaigns for the worldwide repeal of blasphemy laws:

> Atheists are often charged with blasphemy, but it is a crime that they cannot commit. When the Atheist examines, denounces or satirises the gods, *he is not dealing with persons, but with ideas*. He is incapable of insulting God because he does not admit the existence of any such being.

In his posthumously published *Open Letter*, the murdered *Charlie Hebdo* caricaturist Stéphane Charbonnier, known as Charb, makes exactly the same point: 'A non-believer, no matter how hard he tries, cannot blaspheme.' In his public response to the *Charlie Hebdo* murders, French prime minister Manuel Valls declared that French citizens must continue to blaspheme 'to show that in France blasphemy does not exist'. The key ideas here are (a) that hurting ideas, ideologies, or beliefs has nothing to do with hurting people or real bodies (as Foote put it, there is no need to be 'tender about ghosts'); and (b) because the gods do not exist, blasphemy cannot exist.

This is a different view from the story of Naboth's vineyard. For modern atheists and secularists there is no such thing as 'blasphemy' in any circumstances. 'Blasphemy' is always in inverted commas, and so are 'god' and 'religion'. For the biblical author, genuine blasphemy may exist, but definitely not in Naboth's case. The accusation of blasphemy is fake; but the true God, who punishes the fake charge of blasphemy in the name of truth, certainly exists.

In the early 20th century, writers such as G. K. Chesterton and T. S. Eliot penned striking obituaries for blasphemy (which are, like all obituaries for blasphemy, premature). In *Heretics* (1905), Chesterton declared:

> Blasphemy...depends upon a philosophical conviction. Blasphemy depends upon belief and is fading with it. If any one doubts this, let him sit down seriously and try to think blasphemous thoughts about Thor. I think his family will find him at the end of the day in a state of some exhaustion.

In *After Strange Gods: A Primer on Modern Heresy* (1934), Eliot famously announced:

> [Blasphemy] is a very different thing in the modern world from what it would be in an 'age of faith'...No one can possibly blaspheme in any sense except that in which *a parrot may be said to curse*, unless he profoundly believes in what he profanes.

Eliot and Chesterton agree (and so would George Foote) that a true blasphemy *can only be committed by believers*. Both agree, too, that you can only blaspheme against a god/idea in which you truly believe. The comedian Stewart Lee makes a similar point in his documentary *Don't Get me Started: What's Wrong with Blasphemy?*, made in response to the blasphemy protests led by the organization Christian Voice against his musical *Jerry Springer: The Opera* in 2005. In one segment, Lee interviews Alan Moore, an earnest believer from Northampton, who worships Glycon, the snake-god of the Roman Empire, in his garden shed. How hilarious to imagine that you can blaspheme against Thor or Glycon, Ishtar or Wotan, in 21st-century Britain. To add to the joke, Glycon is the 'god' that the Roman satirist Lucian outed as a fake.

Chesterton and Eliot both agree that a *true* blasphemy must amount to more than upsetting social convention and good manners. Eliot mocks a world where people utter 'blasphemies', with no feeling, like *parrots*, while the moral majority goes through the motions of being shocked by 'any public impertinence towards a Deity for whom [they] privately feel no respect at all'. According to Eliot, people no longer believe in gods or the royal family, but keep up appearances in good manners and habits of respect. He also argues that blasphemy is no longer possible because the old gods have been replaced by 'economic determinism' as the new 'god before whom we fall down and worship'. This is a striking observation, given that Eliot was writing back in 1934.

In a novel twist on the idea of 'blasphemy in scarequotes', Chesterton and Eliot *mourn* the fact that blasphemy has become 'blasphemy', because this signals a loss of commitment and belief. Whereas Eliot thinks of belief in exclusively religious terms, Chesterton includes all philosophical and political convictions, including the beliefs of public atheists and Enlightenment thinkers who fought so hard to remove the 'gags from all the heresies'. Looking back at the passion of people like Richard Carlile, Abner Kneeland, or George Foote, Chesterton comments that 'even atheism is too theological for us to-day' for we have lost our political theological and philosophical 'convictions', 'big ideas and big visions', and 'cries for the moon'. In a hilarious passage, he compares the good old days when people worked for big ideas like 'liberty, equality and fraternity', and there was no 'process' to intervene between people and their objectives, and today (today being 1905), when we are trapped in metadiscourse and calculations of 'efficiency':

> [In the past], if men [*sic*] wanted to kick a man downstairs, they did not say 'Efficiently elevating my right leg using, you will notice, the muscles of the thigh and calf, which are in excellent order, I—'. Their feeling was quite different. They were so filled with the beautiful vision of the man lying flat at the foot of the staircase that in that ecstasy the rest followed in a flash…

Chesterton laments the lost immediacy of such automatic, reflex reactions. Using a similar metaphor, a contemporary Christian writer, writing in the 1970s, describes the visceral reaction to a blasphemy as 'the feeling that one gets when his [*sic*] house is broken into' or 'the righteous indignation' that wells up when 'someone touches your most serious psychological nerves'. Chesterton and Eliot's comments on the new gods of economy and the deadening force of 'efficiency' seem strangely timely. They seem newly relevant in these times of 'post-truth', where many lament the loss of politics, the big idea: the idea for which we would write, or act, or kick—or even die.

G. K. Chesterton also raises another important question—recently revived by scholars such as Robert Yelle and David Tollerton. Are there 'secular sacreds' and therefore 'secular blasphemies'? What's the difference, really, between an abused Qur'an or a 'blasphemous' crucifixion and violations of the Holocaust or attacks on that square of holy cloth, the flag? Can the media's sometimes gauche efforts to pixillate offensive cartoons of Muhammad be compared to *The Guardian*'s respectful refusal to show the public lynching of George Floyd, or debates about the ethics of showing photographs of the dead body of the child refugee Aylan Kurdi? Can we and should we separate the brutal crimes by the Saudi regime against Jamal Khashoggi from those against Raif Badawi or Ashraf Fayadh? Would it be useful to compare the effects of blasphemy laws, banning certain words, names, and gestures, to the censorial effects of Google and China's internet search engine *Dragonfly*, obliterating searches for (sacred) words like 'religion' and 'human rights'? Are some people offended by *Monty Python's Life of Brian*'s famous song 'Always Look on the Bright Side' (while others use it as a soundtrack for family funerals) because of the mockery of torture and human suffering and/or because of the mockery of Christ?

From the conviction of James Nayler for actions 'derogatory to the honour of God, and destructive to humane Society', blasphemy has always blurred sacred things and the community/society. Ethno-nationalism is clearly a major factor in many contemporary blasphemy prosecutions, which often target ethnic and religious minorities. Is there really such a difference between the removal of Maqbool Fida Husain's *Bharat Mata*/Mother India (a map of India as a naked female) from the Asia Gallery in London in 2007, and the Tate Gallery's removal, in 2005, just after the London bombings, of John Latham's artwork *God is Great*? Or is there only a technical difference: only one is officially 'blasphemous' because only one mentions God by name?

Chapter 3
Blasphemy and religion

In 2005, just after the 7 July bombings in London, John
Latham's artwork *God is Great* (a New Testament, a Torah,
and a Qur'an spliced by a broken pane of glass) was hastily
removed from an exhibition at the Tate gallery in London.
Representatives of the Muslim Council of Great Britain
protested that they had not been consulted, and highlighted
the dangers of projecting the hurt feelings of religious
communities, then protecting them in advance by withdrawing
potentially controversial art. They argued that these kinds of
'protective' gestures played into the hands of those (Muslims
and others) who wanted modern Islam to be dominated by
neo-fundamentalist Islam.

Talking about *God is Great*, John Latham described the Talmud,
Bible, and Qur'an as representing 'non-negotiable...belief
systems'. Introductions to blasphemy not written by religion
specialists often make simplistic declarations that (and this is a
direct quote from an otherwise excellent book) blasphemy was a
'single and well-defined act' in some old religious past. Statements
like these show how complex texts and interpretative traditions
have been taken over by the *public image* of 'the Bible' or 'the
Qur'an'.

Can blasphemy be applied to non-theistic religions?

If the simplistic dictionary definition of blasphemy as 'profane speaking of God or sacred things' is correct, then it follows that blasphemy can only apply to theistic religions (religions with a God figure) or religions that draw a clear line between the sacred and the profane.

Scholars of religion have often pointed out that the very idea of religion has been organized around Christian concepts, into which other religions and global philosophies cannot easily be squeezed. Not all 'religions' have a personal and transcendent God figure, or are so concerned with right belief and correct words about God, or make firm distinctions between the holy and the everyday. Philosopher Jacques Derrida describes religion as a European-Christian concept that speaks 'Greek and Latin' and has been exported across the world.

Blasphemy would appear to be a very good example of this. It is a Greek word (*blasphēmía*) that spread with the Roman empire when Christianity became the official religion of Rome. It then had a new lease of life after the Protestant Reformation, because Protestants started to use the term 'blasphemy' to distinguish themselves from Catholics, who used the word 'heresy' (meaning wrong religious *ideas*, wrong content, or beliefs at odds with orthodox teaching—but often blurring, in practice, with blasphemy, as we shall see in Chapter 4). Many of the global blasphemy laws were British exports, including the Massachusetts law that convicted Abner Kneeland, the blasphemy laws in Canada, New Zealand, and Australia, and the Indian Penal Code which laid the foundation for the contemporary blasphemy laws in India, Bangladesh, and Pakistan.

Whereas the British blasphemy law only protected Anglican Christianity right up until its abolition in 2008, the Indian Penal

Code, established by the British empire, was designed for a multireligious context where (as Salman Rushdie quips in *The Satanic Verses*) 'the human population outnumbers the divine by less than three to one'. The original code of 1860, drawn up by the Whig politician Thomas Babington Macaulay, was the first code to establish the crime of 'insult[ing] religious *beliefs*'—plural. The revised code of 1927 defined blasphemies as 'Deliberate and malicious acts, intended to outrage religious feelings of any class of citizens in India by insulting its religion or religious beliefs'. Only much later would this idea of protecting religions plural be imported back to some European countries, where it was often awkwardly added on to laws originally designed to protect Christianity, exclusively.

In Britain, the 'Indian penal code solution' was often proposed in debates on abolishing or reforming the blasphemy laws. But the solution was roundly rejected on the grounds that not all religions were equal and equally deserving of social reverence and respect. Home Office memos from the first half of the 20th century, carefully documented by social historian David Nash, are rude reminders of times when what we now term racial and religious discrimination (and blindness to racial and religious discrimination) was normative. Officials declared that Hinduism was 'hardly worthy of the name of religion' and made the circular argument that '*if* it were shown that aspersions on the Jewish religion were regular occurrences, a case could be made for extending the blasphemy laws' (my emphasis). When the secularist George Foote made his famous declaration that there could be no such thing as blasphemy in the 1880s, he also argued that the Christian deity deserved no more respect/reverence than the 'bloodthirsty, tribal' God of the Jews, the 'Brahamanic or Mohammedan' gods, or 'Mumbo Jumbo' (the colonial term for a meaningless African god or ritual). The activist atheist campaigned for the abolition of blasphemy by arguing that Christianity was *just as bad* as the lower-status religions of the 'Brahmins', the 'Mohammedans', the Africans, and the Jews.

Can the Greek-Christian concept of blasphemy be exported and translated into other religions and global philosophies? Or is asking a Hindu or a Buddhist, 'What is your perspective on blasphemy?' rather like asking, 'What's your word for the theistic God?' or 'Who is your Jesus?' or 'Where is your Bible?' Some specialists argue that 'blasphemy' is a British-Christian import that is entirely foreign to Hindu tradition. Hinduism lacks some of the crucial ingredients for blasphemy. There are many gods—not one—and the gods are not jealous. The divine reality exists, but the gods do not punish human actions. Hurting gods, therefore, is an alien concept. And though the truism that Hinduism is more about *orthopraxy* (doing the right thing) than *orthodoxy* (saying or believing the right thing) is easily overstated, it is certainly true that there is nothing like the Christian idea of divine punishment for hurtful or doctrinally offensive speech.

But if we dig deeper, it seems that comparisons can be found. While the gods themselves do not suffer from, or react to, human insult, offences against the gods *can* be a problem insofar as the deities are aligned with particular families or regions. In 1992, Hindu activists destroyed the Ayodhya mosque in the birthplace of the Hindu deity Rama. In Chapter 1, we saw that dictionaries often associate blasphemy with profanation or sacrilege, and Hinduism is very concerned with impurity and the profanation of temples and sacred spaces. Wendy Doniger, whose book *The Hindus: An Alternative History* was at the centre of a major blasphemy controversy, makes the important point that the idea of *social* blasphemy is very strong in Hinduism, even as there is less emphasis on blasphemy as an offence against the gods.

Central to Hinduism is the concept of *dharma*: an expansive word meaning duty, religion, proper ritual, morality, social obligations, justice, righteousness, and law. Traditional Hindu thought is deeply concerned with *adharma*: non-dharma or anti-dharma. *Adharma* includes offensive speech by members of lower castes against people of higher castes, and especially abusive speech against the highest religious authorities, the Brahmins. Though Sanskrit scholar Patrick Olivelle points out that many of the punishments were never carried out in practice, the laws of Manu from the 2nd century BCE list horrific punishments for a 'man of low birth' who hurls 'cruel words' upwards:

> If a man of low birth hurls cruel words at a Brahmin, his tongue should be cut out. If he mentions his name or caste maliciously, a red-hot iron nail ten-fingers long should be thrust into his mouth. If he is so proud as to instruct Brahmins about their duty, the king should have hot oil poured into his mouth and ears.

> (*Manu* 8.270–3).

Mutilations of the mouth (hot oil poured into the mouth, and cutting the tongue) are uncannily like the horrific defacing of the Quaker James Nayler in 1656 (see Chapter 1). The *Arthashastra* of Kautilya, the textbook of politics from the same period as the laws of Manu, suggests a much lighter punishment. Only a fine should be imposed on the man who says, for example, 'Vile Brahmin!' (*AS* 3.18.7).

In Buddhism, as in Hinduism, there is no theological blasphemy, but there is social blasphemy. Buddha is not a god and, according to *Garava Sutta*, the enlightened ones are *above* pain including emotional/social pain. The *Bodhicaryāvatāra* teaches that 'hatred of those who damage sacred images and stupas [sacred buildings] or abuse the true teaching is inappropriate, since the Buddhas and Bodhisattvas are not distressed' (verse 64). But, in his famous awakening under the Banyan tree, the Buddha reflects that human beings have their being in the social sphere of 'reverence or deference', which is essential to their existence. Since the Buddha himself has no human superior to revere, he will revere the *dhamma* (dharma). But other human beings on the path to enlightenment must revere the Brahmins. There are numerous warnings for those who are 'obdurate and haughty', who 'revile the Noble Ones', who 'do not pay homage to whom he should pay homage, or rise up for whom he should rise up, or give a seat to whom he should give a seat, or make way for whom he should make way, or worship him who should be worshipped, or respect him who should be respected, or honour him who should be honoured'. These bad *kammas* will lead to rebirth in the lower realms of the animal or hungry ghost.

In her brilliant book on world religions, Tomoko Masuzawa shows how European and American scholars constructed a hierarchy of world religions, with Christianity at the top, giving different world religions different characteristics. From the 19th century onwards, Buddhism was seen positively, as peace-loving and close to Christianity, whereas Islam, like Judaism, was seen as a problem religion, associated with religious violence and strict adherence to the law. The public images of world religions act as a filter for world events. A relatively benign public image of Buddhism might explain why many automatically think of blasphemy as a Muslim problem, while few are aware of the charges of heresy (*adhamma*) and malpractice (*avinaya*) brought against Buddhist monks in Myanmar. In 2012, the KBO (Knowing Buddha Organization), also known as the Dharma Army, was established to protest against disrespectful treatment of the Buddha. Unlike the body and face of Muhammad, the body and face of Buddha are often treated with affection in North America and Europe, and appropriated for decoration and branding. Many are surprised when the naive use of ritual objects and smiling (easy-going?) Buddhas causes offence.

Human gods

Wendy Doniger makes a very important point when she shows how blasphemy is a relevant concept for Hinduism (and also Buddhism) if it is understood as a social concept, tied to the maintenance of *dharma*. What she misses—and what everyone misses—is the similarity between this understanding of blasphemy and blasphemy in Judaism and Christianity. The God of the Hebrew Bible/Old Testament is often shockingly human or anthropomorphic. He is vulnerable to and insulted by others—as of course is the incarnate son of God, crucified like a criminal on the cross.

The Hebrew words that were later translated using the Greek word 'blasphemy' mean 'to insult', 'to abuse', 'to revile', 'to despise', 'to curse', 'to defame', and 'to speak injuriously'. One verb, *qillel*, comes from the root 'to make little': literally, to belittle. Another verb, *nakob*, comes from the root 'to pierce'. This verb takes us back to the etymology of blasphemy: 'words that hurt'—or as Socrates, Jesus, or the Cynics might put it, words that bite or sting.

Blasphemy is a visceral, *social* concept, focused on harm to the face, body, or name. Blasphemy is about words that prick, or pierce, or poke at humans or gods. And in the Bible, exactly the same verbs—such as *qillel*, *nakob*, and *blasphēmía*—are used of gods and human beings. The New Testament contains statements such as 'When reviled, we bless; when persecuted, we endure; when *blasphemed* we speak kindly' (1 Corinthians 4:12–13; my emphasis); 'They are surprised that you no longer join them in the same excesses of dissipation, and so they *blaspheme* [you]' (1 Peter 4:4; my emphasis); or 'Blaspheming them (Paul and Barnabas) they contradicted them' (Acts 13:45). By using words like 'slander' for human targets and keeping 'blasphemy' for the divine, translators often (but not always) cover over the fact that blasphemy is used for god and human beings, and *comes from imagining gods as if they were (like) human beings*. Note, too, the fuzzy definition of 'blasphemy' in these examples. Blasphemy can mean, simply, saying bad words about, or contradicting, someone, taking a different view. And we've all met people and have heard of gods who can feel 'blasphemed' by others not sharing the same practices or convictions, or taking a different view.

Those who study blasphemy from other disciplines such as law or history often assume that once-upon-a-religious-time, blasphemy was simple and somehow purely religious, focused on 'God or sacred things'. The old religious times are often used as a contrast to modern times, when blasphemy became more of a 'social' concept, concerned with protecting social and moral order and religious communities. But blasphemy was never a purely 'religious' category, as it is often imagined to be. The concept came from imagining the gods as social beings, exposed to war, strife, love (and hate), and difficult relationships with their people and other gods.

Sometimes speakers in the Hebrew Bible/Old Testament address their God in terms that seem, to modern ears, rude and disrespectful, even blasphemous, when they urge God not to sleep, to help, to do something *for God's sake*. Literally for God's sake. Literally for God's sake. God's reputation is tied to his people's social status. If his people are humiliated, then his God-value index will fall in the eyes of other gods and other groups. If for no other reason, he must protect his people for the sake of his reputation, for his good name is tied to the community's good name (Joshua 7:9; Jeremiah 14:21; Ezekiel 20:22; Psalm 74:10, 18). In the Bible, blasphemy can also mean 'anything that we do or say that causes us, and our god, to be disrespected or mocked by other groups'. When King David forces the married woman, Bathsheba, to have sex with him, then has her husband murdered, this is described by God and his prophet as 'blasphemy' against the good name of the community. In a more uncomfortable biblical example, the author of the New Testament books of 1 Timothy and Titus argues that slaves should submit to their masters and women should submit to men so that the good name of Christianity won't be *blasphemed* by the Romans. In this example, blasphemy is a conservative concept. Preventing blasphemy is about preserving the status quo.

The Ten Commandments and the name

Blasphemy has its origins in the theistic, anthropomorphic religions of West Asia (a more appropriate term for what used to be called the Middle East). To blaspheme is to give someone, or some god, a bad name: to blacken someone's name and therefore damage someone's very person, for according to the ancient cultures of West Asia the name *is* the person, and power and life is in the name. In a text from the Nineteenth Dynasty in Egypt (*c.*1350–1200 BCE), the goddess Isis says to the god Re: 'Say to me your name, my divine father, for a man lives when one recites his name.' According to Exodus 22:28, 'You shall not blaspheme God or curse a leader of your people.' God sits alongside the other names that are big and so in particular danger of being belittled. The old religious laws are concerned with protecting the high and holy names: Gods, Brahmins, and kings. *Women, slaves, and those who are already low down in the social pecking order cannot be blasphemed.* In Exodus 22:28, God and the human leader reinforce one another, and collectively represent order and authority. Blasphemy is the offence of 'doing wrong to majesty or sovereignty', known as the crime of *lèse-majesté*.

What does it mean to protect the name? Here are the two of the Ten Commandments that relate to blasphemy:

> You shall not make for yourself a *pesel* [sculpture/statue/idol] whether in the form of anything that is in heaven above, or that is on the earth beneath...You shall not bow down to them or worship them; for I the Lord your God am a jealous God.

> You shall not make wrongful use of the name of the Lord your God, for the Lord will not acquit anyone who misuses his name.
>
> (Exodus 20:4–5; 7; Deuteronomy 5:8, 11)

There is a maximalist and minimalist reading of both commandments. In the maximalist interpretation, the commandment about images prohibits making images of any living things, for any purpose. Alternatively, and more specifically, it only prohibits making images to *worship* (other gods). There is also another possible interpretation: it is forbidden to make images of the true God because he is beyond representation and cannot be touched or seen. In a minimalist reading of the commandment about the name, it is acceptable to use the name of God in a proper oath (as when Naboth says 'God forbid that I should give you my ancestral inheritance')—just not to *misuse* the name, or use it wrongfully. A maximalist or ultra-safe reading—designed to make sure that the commandment is not broken—bans any mention of the divine name. This is the approach taken in the Gospel narrative of Jesus's trial, where Jesus (or the narrator) refers to God as 'the Power'.

These commandments should not be read in isolation, but in the context of many passages about the struggle to represent God, or speaking (and not speaking) the divine name. In Exodus 3:13–15, Moses 'sees' god but only in the form of a miraculously burning bush and the sound of the voice of God coming from the fire. Moses asks God for his name and God replies: 'I am who I am' or 'I will be who I will be': in Hebrew *Yahweh*, written without consonants as the tetragrammaton YHWH.

Try to pronounce the word YHWH out loud, without any vowels to help you. The name cannot be spoken—and this is the point. It can only be expressed through code words such as *Adonai* ('my Lord'), G-d, or *Ha-Shem*, simply meaning 'the name'. Other religions are also famously decorous, or cryptic, around the names of God and holy figures. In Islam, the mention of the name of Muhammad is followed by *alayhi s-salām* or 'Peace be Upon Him', and the name is often represented calligraphically, in a decorated frame. The Hindu *Upanishads* (800–500 BCE) say of the god Indha: 'even though he is really Indha, people cryptically call him Indra because gods in some ways love the cryptic and despise the plain'.

In reporting on the Muhammad cartoons in the Danish Cartoon Affair or *Charlie Hebdo*, many media outlets took the decision to used pixillated photographs or what the BBC termed 'responsible glimpses': images shown for such a brief nanosecond that they could not be processed by the brain. Ancient scriptures may use different media techniques, but they strive for similar effects to represent the sacred figures that cannot/should not be seen. Using only words, the Bible describes how Moses 'saw' God, but only as a burning bush and disembodied voice; or how the prophet Ezekiel glimpsed, through the radiance, God at several removes, like a tenth generation photocopy: 'the *image* of the *likeness* of the *glory* of the Lord' (Ezekiel 1:28; my emphases). In Exodus 33:18–23, Moses asks to see God's face, but God refuses, for no one can see his face and live. However, if Moses hides in the cleft of the rock, God will pass by and cover Moses with his hand, then finally take away his hand after he has passed by so that Moses can see *God's back*.

Try acting out this scene with a friend. Try to put your hands in front of someone else's face, pass them, then show yourself from the back, without your face being seen. It is impossible, even if you are trained in gymnastics or yoga. The very awkward positions taken up by God and Moses in this rather gauche narrative demonstrate the impossibility (but also desirability) of presenting God as a living figure, but also hiding him, at the same time. God has a hand—but the hand is to be used to hide his face. God has a body—but Moses can only see his back.

This Bible story, now largely forgotten, became infamous in the 19th century when it became the butt (so to speak) of blasphemous jokes. John William Gott, the last man to be imprisoned for blasphemy in Britain in the 1920s, quipped that if heaven is God's throne, and earth his footstool, there must be a 'frightful distance between his feet and the part he displayed to Moses on Mount Sinai'. Figure 7 shows George Foote's cartoon 'Moses Getting a Back View', published in the penny newspaper *The Freethinker*.

MOSES GETTING A BACK VIEW.

b 'Exodus xxxiii, 21-3', from the *Freethinker*, Christmas number, 1882

7. 'Moses Getting a Back View', from *The Freethinker*, Christmas 1882 edition.

Clothed in ripped chequered trousers and braces, the deity appears as a common working man, rather than a gentleman. God does not show his back but his backside.

A fundamental paradox in the representation of God leads to two conflicting positions on blasphemy which have battled it out from the very inception of the idea. In the Bible, God is (like) the most elite person in human society; but he is beyond the merely human and entirely above society. Two conflicting conclusions follow. Because he is imagined as the most superior being, like a king, but above the king, God's name and person must be revered above all. But because God is so far above a merely human person, it is offensive ('blasphemous') to dare to imagine that the transcendent God could possibly be hurt or harmed by petty human words and images. The first conclusion supports the idea of regulations and penalties for blasphemy. The second conclusion *undermines* blasphemy and suggests that the very idea of blasphemy can be a blasphemy: an offence to God's divinity. As the Emperor Tiberius famously put it, *Deorum injuriae diis curae* ('let the gods defend their own honour' or 'The gods can protect themselves'). Gods are far too godlike to need a Divine Defence League.

For centuries, the idea of *blasphemous libel* (which is actually a legal concept) has been mocked by comedians and campaigners for legal reform. How can a god be libelled? On what basis can we prove whether a statement is true or false (libellous)? In the 1720s, the convicted blasphemer Thomas Woolston wittily pointed out that by 'calling on the Civil Magistrate for [God's] Aid and Assistance' the state seems to be admitting that the God of Christianity is not very God-like. Supporting the repeal of the 1819 French blasphemy law in 1881, Georges Clemenceau argued that 'God will take care of himself. He does not need the *Chambre des députés* to defend him.' Across the channel in Britain, also in the 1880s, looking at the 'wordy jumble' of the twenty-eight folios and sixteen counts in his Indictment (which he had to pay for, in order to obtain a copy of the charges against him), George Foote joked that it was 'highly presumptuous' and 'impertinent' on the 'part of weak men to defend the character of Almighty God'. Had his prosecutors learned of God's displeasure in a dream, or had God chosen to whisper his displeasure to them directly? Had he given them power of attorney, and was he ready to be subpoenaed as a witness at the trial?

Contemporary comedians have enjoyed carrying on the old comedy routine. Blasphemy laws are laws 'to protect an all-powerful, supernatural deity from getting its feelings hurt', quips comedian Ricky Gervais. 'Blasphemy is the only victimless crime.'

It should be noted, however, that at least since the mid-19th century, law has rarely been so crass as to make blasphemy a crime against soft *divine* sensitivities. In the trial of the English secularist and newspaper editor George Holyoake (convicted in

1842 for comments made at a public lecture at the Cheltenham Mechanics' Institute) the judge, Mr Justice Erskine, said, 'We do not presume to be protective of our God, but to protect the people from such indecent language.' Blasphemy has been gradually secularized, becoming a crime against the public peace, social order, or the feelings of believers. Transforming blasphemy into a *purely* social crime has allowed the idea of blasphemy to survive.

The face of Muhammad

A book with the suggestive title *Figurations and Sensations of the Unseen in Judaism, Christianity and Islam* (2019) explores the paradox of touch, sensation, and visualization at the heart of the three monotheistic religions. The three religions want to bring the highest, holiest figures and teachings *close*. They want to sense them and make them tangible and present in images, smells, lights, music, sounds, and words. But at the same time, they strive to convey the special effect or sensation of the holy as inaccessible, invisible, intangible, and set apart. One of the contributors to the book, historian of Islamic art Christiane Gruber, describes this as the paradox of *real absence*. God is beyond the senses and imagination and/but God is close, present, and the Opener of Eyes.

Even more than in Judaism, and certainly Christianity, God is beyond figuration in Islam. To present Allah as human is to commit the sin of *shirk* (idolatry). The Qur'an warns, 'Do not associate others with God; to associate is a mighty wrong' (Q 31.13). But the Qur'an also states that 'It is not for any mortal that God should speak to him except by revelation or from behind a veil' (Q 42.51–2).

As Ibrahim Moosa explains, Muhammad is the 'symbolic sovereign, higher than any earthly sovereign'. The figure and person of the prophet is 'coterminous with the identity of the Muslim community', known as the *umma*. Because the presence of the Prophet is embodied in the men responsible for his *political* and *religious* legacy, crimes of insulting the Prophet blur into offences concerned with disturbing religious teaching and threatening the peace of the state. Arabic terms for personal insult against the Prophet, such as *shatm* or *sabb al-rasul* ('insult to the messenger') and *hijā* (satire, lampoon, invective, abuse) easily merge into crimes of unbelief, such as *riddah* or *irtidad* (apostasy) and *takfir* (anathema; proclaiming someone to be an unbeliever or *kafir*). To insult the Prophet is to harm the community and the solidarity of the *umma* and to cause *fitnah*: disunity, chaos, and civil unrest.

Without overstretching the comparisons, we can see a common theme emerging across the world religions. In Islam, 'blasphemy' is about protecting the community from *fitnah*. In Hinduism and Buddhism it is about preventing *adharma*. In the Bible, blasphemy is a crime of *lèse-majesté*, concerned with protecting the dignity of socially revered gods and men. In each case, blasphemy is social, political, and religious, and prohibiting blasphemy is about protecting community cohesion. This is strangely similar to the understanding of blasphemy in modern secular law, where (as we will see in more detail in Chapter 4) blasphemy blurs into heresy, sedition, libel (and obscenity), and is often understood as 'outrage to morality', common values, or an attack on the public peace.

Recent protests over 21st-century cartoons of Muhammad have led journalists and non-specialists to ask what the Muslim position has been on representing Muhammad's body and face. The answer is that, while there is a strong tendency towards hiding the face of Muhammad, there is no single position in the multivalent traditions of Islam. In an exquisite painting of the anointing of the Muhammad in an early fourteenth century Persian manuscript (Rashid al-Din, *Jami' al Tawarikh/ Compendium of Chronicles* 1307–08), the young prophet appears with his face uncovered. But in a 16th-century manuscript also from Iran (Figure 8), Muhammad's face is veiled.

Lengthy *verbal* descriptions of Muhammad's face, appearance, and character can also be found in some of the hadith traditions (authoritative traditions about Muhammad's words and actions). In Ottoman Turkey, these verbal descriptions were used for devotion and protection and were displayed on calligraphic *hilya* ('ornament') panels. One popular hadith tells how two visitors from Mecca were

8. A veiled Muhammad kneels as he speaks to God, represented as a burst of golden flame; Iranian manuscript, 1570–1.

absolutely astonished when the Byzantine Emperor Heraclius showed them a portrait of Muhammad in a drawer in his cabinet of portraits of the prophets. The lesson of the hadith is ambiguous. The portrait exists—but its existence causes shock and surprise.

The majority of representations of Muhammad's face and body come from Persia and Turkey between 1200 and 1600 CE, in illustrated manuscripts intended for elite, private audiences, or from modern Iran. Shi'a Islam has been far more open to the representation of Muhammad and sacred figures than Sunni Islam. Before Shi'a traditions were attacked by the Pahlavi king, Reza Shah Pahlavi (1878–1944), visual representations of Muhammad and his family and other Shi'ite saints were common, in paintings, lithograph prints, photographs, and wall paintings. A mural of Muhammad's night journey, with Muhammad's face blank, was painted in Tehran in 2008. Numerous postcards and posters depict the face and figure of Imam Ali, the successor to Muhammad in Shi'a Islam.

Focusing on whether Muhammad's face is blank, veiled, or visualized might well be a distraction—a question set by European and American journalists rather than a question that emerges from inside Islam. The 14th-century Iranian painting of the anointing of Muhammad, where Muhammad's face is shown, uses all the senses—an angel pouring incense and worshippers and animals on their knees—to create a sensation of the exceptional status of the young Muhammad. Aesthetically, it is very *similar* to the 16th-century manuscript (Figure 8), where God 'appears' to a veiled Muhammad (as he appears to Moses) as a burning flame, a great ball of light, and the two presences are alone in the heavens (in the original colour version, a gorgeous burst of the most precious colours of lapis blue and gold). As with white, blonde European Jesuses and beautiful Virgin Marys, all the conventions of beauty are used to portray the face of Imam Ali. Veiled or unveiled, holy faces and figures are defined by aesthetic perfection. Holiness is synonymous with beauty while profanation/blasphemy is expressed in ugliness and vulgar caricature.

Blasphemy and religious violence

Anyone who has watched the 'blasphemous' Monty Python film *Life of Brian* will probably remember the scene where Brian (the unfortunate doppelgänger for Jesus) and his not very glamorous mother Mandy go to watch the stoning of Matthias, son of Deuteronomy of Gath, presided over by the high priest (John Cleese). Poor Matthias has only blasphemed by accident. As he says in his defence: 'All I said to my wife was, "That piece of halibut was good enough for Jehovah".' But High Priest Cleese is an example of those 'ones-who-are-(extremely)-sensitive-to-blasphemy' (discussed in Chapter 2). He refuses to make any distinction between accidental and deliberate blasphemy. In a perfect irony, Cleese himself then blasphemes by accident ('I'm warning you. If you say "Jehovah" once more...') and is promptly pelted with stones, which he cannot stop, even though he tries to call time on his execution by blowing a whistle, like a referee.

Monty Python's Life of Brian's death-by-stoning scene runs the risk of supporting the popular myth that people were regularly stoned for blasphemy in some retro-religious past. In fact there are only four cases of execution for blasphemy in the Bible—Naboth, Jesus, and Stephen (the three cases discussed in Chapter 2), and an unnamed man in Leviticus 24—and, of these, three out of four executions are clearly a mistake. In Leviticus 24, a man who is a half-foreigner 'blasphemes the Name in a curse' by accident, during a fight (but it does not matter that he blasphemes by accident, any more than intention to blaspheme matters in two-thirds of contemporary global blasphemy laws). The story is all about protecting community purity from danger; discharging the danger of blasphemy like an electric current through the poor man's body. The half-foreign man who has blasphemed is taken outside the camp. All who have heard the blasphemy place their hands upon his head and then stone him to death.

The horrific story in Leviticus 24 is not the Old Testament view, and certainly not the 'Jewish' one—though the Christian association of the Jews with the ones-who-are-so-sensitive-to-blasphemy-that-they-crucified-Jesus has often led Christian-majority cultures to assume that 'the Jews' regularly stoned people to death. A very different view is expressed in the foundational book of Jewish law and culture, the Talmud: the book that was often burnt for blasphemy in medieval and early modern Europe, having been charged with 'blasphemies' against Jesus and Mary and 'foolish and revolting tales'. The structure of the Talmud is rather like discussion threads on the internet. Famous rabbis present *different* opinions. The tractate (or discussion thread) called *Sanhedrin* goes to great lengths to make blasphemy an exceptional, and even impossible, offence.

According to the Talmud, a blasphemer is *only* guilty if he has cursed the tetragrammaton (Yhwh) specifically. He must have uttered the blasphemy at least twice, to make sure that this is not an accident. The rabbis contributing to this compilation of Jewish law are well aware of the problem of accidental blasphemy, as in the case of poor Matthias in the *Life of Brian*. One rabbi insists that in order to be convicted of blasphemy, a 'blasphemer' must have said, very precisely, 'May Yhwh smite Yhwh': a statement that no one could possibly make by accident! The writers of the Talmud actually put the offence in code as 'May José smite José'. This is because to write the words 'curse God' would be to repeat the blasphemy and get into the same kind of pickle as John Cleese's high priest. For the same reason, the Hebrew term for blasphemy, *ḥillul-ha-shem* (desecrating the Name) is written in code as *birkat ha-shem*: 'blessing the Name'. In this long discussion thread, another rabbi adds the point that the commandment is only for Jews, not gentiles. And another rabbi comments: 'He who hears the Divine Name blasphemed nowadays need not rend his garments, for otherwise one's garments would be reduced to tatters.' The sense seems to be: 'You will never get rid of blasphemy. Were we to over-react most of the population would be dead.'

In the Bible, blasphemy is prohibited and necessary (as in the case of Jesus); genuine and fake (as in the case of Naboth); and forgiveable and unforgiveable (Matthew 12. 31-32). It is a theological, *and* a social-communal, offence. The right response is to do nothing, to turn the other cheek, and, only in one case, to kill. Draconian punishments for religious dissent in contemporary Muslim states such as Saudi Arabia, Pakistan, and Iran stand in contrast to early Islam and the teaching of the Qur'an. One verse in the Qur'an declares that apostates will suffer an unspecified punishment in hell (Q 9.74), but another emphasizes pardon and forgiveness (Q 2.109).

None of the 6.326 verses of the Qur'an prescribe silencing 'blasphemy' by force. Many statements advocate non-retaliation against those who utter 'noxious talk' or 'make sport' of religion, for wise theological, social and psychological reasons. God alone can deal with blasphemy. By not retaliating, victims avoid increasing their own pain by dwelling on the insult. Non-retaliation also de-escalates conflict, and preserves the social peace. Examples include, 'Even though you are sure to hear much that is hurtful, being steadfast and mindful of God is the best course' (Q 3.186); or 'do not sit with' those who 'ridicule God's revelations' (Q 4.140); or 'And when they hear ill speech, turn away from it and say, "For us are our deeds, and for you are your deeds. Peace be upon you"' (Q 28.5); or 'be patient over what they say and avoid them with gracious avoidance' (Q 73.10; cf. 25.63; 33.48; 109.1–6). Q 6.108 exhorts Muslims not to mock other religions, because this will lead to retaliation and blasphemy against Islam.

The *sunna* (the traditions about Muhammad written down in the hadith, which form the basis of much of *Shari'a*) contain detailed stories of retribution that are lacking in the Qur'an. Multivalent hadith traditions include stories of the Prophet putting the Jewish poet Ka'ab bin al-Ashraf to death for having 'hurt' the Prophet (a story told in one of the most authoritative hadith collections, *Sahih al-Bukhari*). While there are no penalties for apostasy (*riddah* or *irtidad*) set out in the Qur'an, in this hadith (and others like it) Muhammad makes the statement 'Whoever changes their religion shall be killed'. The story of the execution of Ka'ab bin al-Ashraf laid the foundation for the influential judgment of the 14th-century jurists Taqi al-Din Ibn Taymiya (d. 1328), and Taqi al-Din al-Subki (d. 1355) that the crime of *sabb al-rasul*, insulting the Prophet, constituted a major sin in Islam, deserving death.

As with the Bible, the Talmud, and the Laws of Manu, there seems to have been a significant gap between laws prescribing corporal and capital punishments and their actual implementation in the history of Islam. The fact that violent punishments are rarely attested in the historical sources has led several scholars to argue that the written laws were intended more as warning and deterrence. Harsh punishments, in written form, are often qualified by loopholes, just as in the Talmud. However, Sunni and Shi'a schools of Islamic jurisprudence now tend to agree on the necessity of some form of punishment for Muslims who commit the crime of *sabb al-rasul*, understood as attacking the body of the community, and bringing about *fitnah* (civil unrest), although opinions on penalties and categories vary between schools.

There have been, and continue to be, mixed legal views on whether non-Muslims who insult Muhammad deserve punishment. In their response to the Danish cartoons in 2005/2006 (see Chapter 5), the Muslim Brotherhood based their principle of non-retaliation on Muhammad's statements: 'He who hurts a dhimmi [non-Muslim/protected person] hurts me' or 'Whoever hurts a dhimmi, I am his adversary' (At-Tabarani; Al-Khatib). When he issued his famous fatwa during the *Satanic Verses* affair, Ayatollah Khomeini famously took the opposite view. Khomeini's view came to dominate the Western public image of Islam, as well as the extremist interpretation of Islam by Wahhabi Islam and Daesh/Isis.

When thinking about blasphemy and hate speech, we should not forget the precedents set by intra-religious blasphemies: insults hurled *between* religions. In his *Inquiry into the Nature of the Sin of Blasphemy* (1817), the Unitarian clergyman Robert Aspland made the point that ridicule is 'not the peculiar property of infidelity and profaneness' since the God of the Bible regularly compares foreign gods to (and this is a literal quote) 'lumps of shit'. Many European churches and cathedrals display humiliated *Synagoga* (Synagogue) next to her triumphant sister, *Ecclesia* (Church). Some also have a *Judensau*: Jews suckling on the giant body of a female pig. In the light of the very public debate about what to do about Confederate flags or statues commemorating colonizers and slave-owners, we should also be discussing what to do with shamed figures of Synagoga and Jews sucking on pigs.

'Blasphemous' modern caricatures of holy figures find an early prototype in the mass-produced woodcuts of the Reformation and Counter-Reformation. Protestants and Catholics did not mince their words, or their images. Monks and Reformers appeared with monstrous, half-animal bodies. The Pope was parodied as a donkey, like Alexamenos's Jesus (see Chapter 1). In *Against the Murderer of Dresden*, the famous Reformer, Martin Luther, went so far as to say that he could not bless without cursing the papists: 'I am unable to pray without at the same time cursing. If I am prompted to say "Hallowed be Thy name", I must add "Cursed, damned, and outraged be the name of the papists..."' In a Reformation cartoon (see Figure 9)—which can be seen as a prototype of contemporary blasphemous cartoons—protesting Protestants fart in the face of the Pope and set his false books and doctrines on fire, while the caption reads, 'Don't frighten us Pope, with your ban, and don't be such a furious man. Otherwise we shall turn around and show you our rears.'

Inner-religious blasphemy

On a recent trip to Barcelona, my son and I were surprised to discover a character called *El Caganer* (literally 'the pooper') with his trousers down, in the middle of a Christmas nativity. It turns

PAPA LOQVITVR.

Sententiæ nostræ etiam iniustæ
metuendæ sunt.

Responsio.

maledicta

Aspice nudatas gens furiosa nates.
Ecco qui Papa el mio bel uedere.

9. Farting and mooning at the Pope in the early blasphemous
Reformation cartoon 'Kissing the Pope's Feet'. From a series of
woodcuts (1545) usually referred to as the *Papstspotbilder* or
Papstspottbilder by Lucas Cranach, commissioned by Martin Luther.

out that he is such a fixed feature that, when the council of
Barcelona commissioned a nativity scene without him (because
he was setting a bad example of public defecation and urination!),
many protested that this was an insult to Catalonian

national traditions. El Caganer is one of many examples of something that so often drops out of contemporary discussions of blasphemy: *inner-religious blasphemy*; mocking and subverting one's own religious traditions.

Today it is common to think in terms of taking up a self-conscious position in relation to religion: choosing to be a believer; choosing to be an atheist, etcetera. Before the mid-1850s, few were thinking of themselves as believers or non-believers, or deliberately blaspheming to argue for the right to be free from religion. But (and probably for this reason) there are many examples of inner-religious blasphemies—mixtures of the sacred and the profane that seem extremely foreign to modern eyes and ears.

In Chapters 1 and 2 we saw how blasphemy was associated with early campaigns for birth control—and then, later, homosexual sex. Because moderns are trained to associate blasphemy with obscenity, we might be confused by earlier religious forms that seem to quite happily blend piety and sex. Hypnotic Sufi devotional music known as *Qawwali*, originating in India in the 13th century, mixes praise of sex and intoxication with the soul's longing for the divine. In a playful passage in the *Arabian Nights*, one male character 'play[s] imam leading the prayer at [the woman's] prayer niche', and she follows him in the postures of prayer, 'the getting up and the sitting down', leading to her final 'outbursts of praise'! Medieval devotional books or books of Psalms often have unexpected 'doodles' in the margins: naked buttocks, monkeys celebrating the eucharist, or even (rather unexpectedly) nuns picking phalluses from a phallus tree. The 11th-century Persian poet Omar Khayyam mocked the hypocrisy of the religious establishment: 'You say rivers of wine flow in heaven, is heaven a tavern to you? You say two *houris* (beautiful women) await each believer there, is heaven a brothel to you?' When the Turkish jazz pianist Fazil Say retweeted these old words in 2013 he was prosecuted for 'insulting religious values': an indictment that was never issued against Omar Khayyam.

Enlightenment thinkers and secularists have often caricatured the old religious believers as docile, obedient children who had not reached the age for grown-up critical thinking. But they also seem to have imagined these children as having no instinct for play. In fact, religious expression can be far more rambunctious, playful, and 'blasphemous' than religion's rather sombre public image, and popular religion has regularly gone off-road, and not always followed the laws and scripts of the writing elites. For example, a medieval Christian performance of that most serious story of the near-sacrifice of Abraham's son in Genesis 22 has Isaac ask his father (who is just about to kill him): 'Have you told my *mum* about this?!' Abraham replies: 'She? Mary's son, Christ forbid!' Abraham's words are faithful to Christian truth. In the traditional symbolism (or typology) of Christianity, Isaac indeed represents Christ who is also Mary's son. But at the same time Abraham's words are a curse and a playful blasphemy: 'Christ forbid…Oh God no!…XXXX No! I couldn't tell her or she would kill me.' The performance is multitonal: simultaneously sacred and profane, serious and hilarious. Isaac's position on the sacrificial altar could not be more serious. But he also raises a smile by asking what his mum might think about her son being offered as a whole burnt offering by his dad.

Blasphemy is *intrinsic* to and even *normative* for religion. This is because so much religious expression depends on the idea that true revelation must upset and even invert linguistic, social, legal, and ethical norms. The Indian mystics known as the *avadhūta* and the *nyönpa* in Tibetan Buddhism are known for upsetting religious etiquette: consuming impure substances, having sex, appearing naked, and pointedly *not* praying and *not* studying. The Jewish rabbi Shabbetai Zvi (1626–76), who came to believe that he was the new messiah, performed what he called 'strange acts' (in Hebrew *ma'asim zari*), including speaking the forbidden name of God out loud. When Zen master Wen-yen was asked by a novice monk, 'What is Buddha?' he answered: 'A dried stick of dung.' During their trial for blasphemy, members of the punk band Pussy

Riot protested that they had been imitating the shocking and unconventional behaviour of Russian Orthodoxy's heretic-saints.

Far from being marginal, the heretic saints and holy fools have been some of the most charismatic and enduring figures in popular religious history. The eccentric, iconoclastic Japanese Zen Buddhist monk and poet Ikkyū (1394–1481), who drank to excess and entered brothels in his religious robes, is the subject of a popular Japanese television series *Ikkyū-san*. The bawdy, rustic, and eloquent clown Marcolf spars with the lofty biblical King Solomon in medieval dialogues that were extremely popular across Europe. Stories of the holy fool and satirist, the 13th-century Turkish sufi Nasreddin, were retold in the 20th-century Azerbaijani satirical periodical *Molla Nasraddin*, widely read across the Muslim world from Morocco to Iran. Most recently, the highest grossing Bollywood film of all time has introduced the world to a new holy fool: the charming alien from outer space known as PK/Peekay (= 'drunk'). As PK tries to take money and coconuts from a Hindu temple into a Christian church, and wine from the Christian eucharist into a mosque, he puzzles over, and almost dies of, what he sees as ridiculous and divisive religious rules. He concludes, like many holy fools before him, that truth lies in transgression, for these religions have misdialled the true God and have a 'wrong number' to spiritual truth. Defiantly, and for some 'blasphemously', the film centres on a Muslim–Hindu love story.

Narendra Modi's Bharatiya Janata party and the influential yoga guru Baba Ramdev denounced *PK* as blasphemous, calling for protests in cinemas, acts of vandalism, and a social boycott of everyone associated with the film.

Chapter 4
Blasphemy and law

The English 'blasphemer' and satirist William Hone (1780–1842) complained that the vagueness of the blasphemy laws reminded him of the tyrant of Syracuse, who wrote his laws high up on the walls in very small letters and then brutally punished those who couldn't read them. He had a point. The former UN Special Rapporteur on freedom of religion or belief, Heiner Bielefeldt, cited the 'inherent vagueness' which 'leaves the whole concept open to abuse' as the main reason for calling, in 2012, for an end to blasphemy laws. The 2017 report *Respecting Rights: Measuring the World's Blasphemy Laws* surveyed the *seventy-one* blasphemy laws across the globe and came to a similar conclusion: blasphemy laws 'are vaguely worded, and few specify or limit the forum in which blasphemy can occur'. The report also placed Italy in the top ten of worst offenders, with exactly the same score as Egypt (though the report also noted the new crackdown on freedom of expression under President Abdel Fatah al-Sisi, unprecedented in Egypt's history). It also revealed other shocking statistics, including the fact that only one-third of blasphemy laws require proof of any intention to blaspheme. This might not be so surprising, if we go back to the definition of blasphemy in Chapter 1. If blasphemy is by definition in the ears and eyes of the receiver, then it follows (logically, but dangerously) that blasphemy laws would be relatively unconcerned with the alleged offender and his/her intention to cause pain.

One of the traditional, more comforting, stories of Enlightenment is the idea that we have gradually escaped from the dangerous absolutism and fuzziness of religion into the relative safety, and clarity, of law. Unfortunately it is not possible to make the history of blasphemy laws fit this pattern. It is impossible to tell a story of the clarification of blasphemy because, to be frank (and frank is what one should be in a *Very Short Introduction*), there really isn't one. Blasphemy is multifaceted and vague in religious traditions—and it is (differently) multifaceted and vague in modern 'secular' law.

In Chapter 3 we saw how, in the Bible and Christian history, blasphemy is social/communal and theological and covers a dizzyingly wide range of offences and responses (from praise to execution!). A blasphemer can be someone who claims miracles; denies miracles; or who commits any act deemed to hurt the good name of the community, an individual person, or a god. In modern secular law, blasphemy has meant all of these things—and more.

Specifically, atheism or secularism has been added to the list. In recent years, blasphemy laws have been used to prosecute Manlio Padovan (a member of the Union of Rational Atheists and Agnostics) for a poster campaign in Italy ('The bad news is that no god exists. The good news is that you don't need one') and Sanal Edamaruku, president of the Indian Rationalist Association, now living in exile in Finland, for mocking miracles by suggesting that the tears of a statue of a weeping Jesus on the cross were really caused by a leaking drain. Blasphemy in the Bible can refer to a *word*, an *object*, or an *act*. Ditto with modern blasphemy laws. In the blasphemy laws of Pakistan, Bangladesh, and India, based on the colonial Indian Penal Code of 1927, blasphemy is defined, but hardly confined, as 'uttering…any word or making any sound or making any gesture or placing…any object in the sight'. Often the same formulae are repeated across the global blasphemy laws. This formula of 'word, sound, gesture, object' is repeated verbatim in contemporary blasphemy laws in a range of countries including (for example) Cyprus, Israel, Jordan, Zambia, Singapore, and Sri Lanka.

Blasphemy and heresy

The prosecutions of Padovan and Edamaruku for atheism or demystifying the miracles of Jesus show that it is still very hard to draw any line between blasphemy; *heresy* (meaning beliefs that endanger orthodox teaching; wrong religious ideas). Blasphemy and heresy also merge in many prosecutions in Muslim states. As we saw in Chapter 3, the identification of the Prophet with the political and religious community means that sins of *riddah* or *irtidad* (apostasy) blur into crimes of insult against the Prophet (*sabb al-rasul*).

The concept of blasphemy underwent a revival when Protestants started to use blasphemy to distinguish themselves from Catholics, who used the word heresy. But the difference was more about religious identity than content. There was no clear distinction from heresy as blasphemy passed from church canon law to common law. Take, for example, the 1650 law passed by Oliver Cromwell's parliament with the fabulous title 'An Act against several Atheistical, Blasphemous and Execrable *Opinions*, derogatory to the honour of God, and destructive to humane Society' (my italics).

The Act seems to define blasphemy by brainstorming all the possible forms of bad behaviour that a tongue and body could get up to. Expansively, blasphemy includes 'swearing profanely or falsely by the Name of God', drunkenness, any form of 'filthy and lascivious speaking', and adultery. Blasphemy is a drunken blur of drinking, swearing, and illicit sex. But having defined blasphemy as every form of immoral life that could possibly be imagined (or fantasized), the law then gives a very specific list of doctrinal sins, directed at a particular set of people. The targets of this law were nonconformist splinter groups such as the Quakers (like

James Nayler), the Sweet Singers of Israel, and the Levellers, Diggers, and Ranters: groups who (like the holy fools, mystics, and messiahs discussed in Chapter 3) believed that true holiness was expressed in 'impure acts' including swearing and breaking laws and conventions about speech and sex.

The 1650 Act shows how easily 'blasphemy' becomes a vehicle for targeting religious minorities—in the past, and in the present. Expansions of the Indian Penal Code in Pakistan since the 1980s have included special clauses directed at Ahmadi Muslims (a group originating in the 19th century, recognizing other prophets after Muhammad). Since even calling themselves Muslims 'outrages the religious feelings of true Muslims', just to be an Ahamadi Muslim is an act of blasphemy, so the logic goes. In Egypt, one of the legal definitions of blasphemy is practising the Baha'i faith. In Iran, followers of the 'false' revelation of Baha'i are punished with execution, torture, imprisonment, social harassment and 'civil disability' (see chapter 2): exclusion from education and employment, confiscation of community assets, and the destruction of holy places and homes.

In order to pinpoint some kind of distinction between blasphemy and heresy, historians and legal scholars often cite the contrast between the Hales judgment of 1676 and the Coleridge judgment of 1883. The Hales judgment refers to the decision of Sir Matthew Hales in 1676 in the case of one John Taylor, a member of the maverick nonconformist Christian group known as the Sweet Singers of Israel who liked to mix sacred lyrics and profane tunes (like Pasolini setting the crucifixion to Carolo Rustichelli's 'Ricotta Twist'). Hales's judgment stated:

> Christianity is parcel of the laws of England, and therefore to
> reproach the Christian religion is to speak in subversion of the law.

In contrast, 200 years later, Lord Coleridge ruled in the trial of the freethinker George Foote (1883):

> If the decencies of controversy are observed, even the fundamentals
> of religion may be attacked, without a person being guilty of
> blasphemous libel.

Hales's definition of blasphemy seems to be in the spirit of Exodus 22:28: 'You shall not blaspheme God or curse a leader of your people.' Blasphemy is any act that can be considered a 'reproach' against the content and the status of the Christian religion. Since there is a very close relation between law, state, and religion, blasphemy is a crime against sovereignty, a crime of *lèse-majesté*.

The Coleridge judgment, in contrast, aims to cut the connection between blasphemy and heresy and between the Christian religion and the state. Finally the distinction between blasphemy and heresy becomes clear. Blasphemy is no longer a matter of 'matter' (content). It is a matter of 'manner' (style). Blasphemy has *always* had a social and political dimension. It has never been purely theological. But the Coleridge judgment emphasized and strengthened this social dimension. Henceforth blasphemy would be a sin against the conversational contract; a crime of bad manners, rudeness, poor taste.

The Coleridge judgment highlights the fact that, up until the 1880s, and arguably much later, blasphemy and offences against the *content* of the Christian religion were hopelessly blurred. It also creates a whole new set of problems by introducing the idea of an invisible decency line that can be crossed—but where exactly, and how? George Foote argued that Coleridge's judgment effectively made blasphemy a class crime, protesting that only a 'parliament of aesthetic gentlemen', perhaps with Mr Oscar Wilde as Prime Minister, could conduct refined blasphemy tests on grounds of taste. In the 19th and 20th centuries such protests became commonplace. Arguing for the repeal of the blasphemy laws in 1924, the Reverend Dr Walter Walsh complained that the laws clearly targeted the 'Hyde Park Orator' who used a verbal 'bludgeon' to attack 'superstition', while protecting any criticism of religion that took the form of a deft and skilful 'stiletto stab in the back' by a 'university don'. Lampooning William Wilberforce's Society for the Suppression of Vice (including the vice of blasphemy), Sydney Smith renamed the organization the Society for Suppressing the Vices of Those Whose Incomes Did Not Exceed £500 a Year.

The Coleridge judgment made explicit what had long been implicit in blasphemy laws. Exorbitant fines meant that the lower classes could be ruined and imprisoned, while gentlemen went unpunished.

In 1663 (in an event recorded in Samuel Pepys's diary), Sir Charles Sedley appeared in public drunk and naked to enact a mock-eucharist and 'excrementize' (the mind boggles). He 'act[ed] all the postures of lust and buggery that could be imagined', then preached a mock-sermon about possessing special sexual powders that would cause all the 'cxxxs' in London to run after him, crazy with lust!. If it is true that you can recognize blasphemy when you see it, this looks like a pretty convincing performance! Sedley was given a dressing down in court, sent to prison for a week, and fined the (then) gigantic sum of £500. He went on to write poetry and sit in the Houses of Parliament. He also became the father of the future mistress of James II. Royalty and the landed gentry have played by different sexual rules, as well as different rules for blasphemy (and the two are often connected, as we saw in Chapter 2).

In contrast, Thomas Woolston, the son of a leatherworker, died in prison in 1721 because he was unable to pay the exorbitant fine of twenty-five pounds per blasphemous publication. By way of rough comparison, one pound equalled twenty shillings; eight shillings would buy a bottle of champagne in Vauxhall; and two shillings and sixpence would get you a whole pig.

Woolston was imprisoned for arguing that the miracles of Jesus must be read allegorically—otherwise they would be ridiculous—and for claiming that Jesus's antics presented him in a not very gentlemanly light. By cursing the fig tree in a petulant fit of rage (Mark 11:12–15), the messiah acted like a tantruming farm labourer. Jesus's question to his mother at the wedding in Cana, 'Woman what have I to do with thee?', was proof of the 'effect of Drinking'—for how else would he not have recognized his mother, if Jesus had not been initiated into the 'Mysteries of Bacchus'? In a similar spirit, the last man to serve a prison sentence for blasphemy in the UK, the socialist trouser salesman John William Gott, quipped that much of the Bible reads as if it had been written in a 'pub' under the 'inspiration of *spirits*'. So often blasphemy involves lowering high and holy characters down into the vernacular, or taking them to the pub. The most shocking thing about Foote's cartoon of the divine posterior (Figure 7, Chapter 3) was probably putting the divine backside in chequered trousers and braces, rather than taking God to a gentleman's outfitters.

Coleridge's judgment officially made blasphemy a matter of tone, class and style—or what historian Steven Shapin terms 'epistemological decorum'. Though he does not write about blasphemy specifically, Shapin's analysis of what he calls the *social history of truth* fits the history of blasphemy laws extremely well. The concept of 'epistemological decorum' means that being accepted as believable and credible has everything to do with decorum (behaviour in keeping with good taste). Shapin's point is that truth is never purely philosophical, any more than blasphemy is ever purely theological. Truth is not just a matter of fact, but a matter of *social fact* or manners. We might be more inclined to believe a gentleman who speaks in a refined male voice, than a woman, or someone who speaks in dialect, non-standard English, or who uses vulgar and improper words.

There is a catch here that 'blasphemers' were quick to exploit. The social conditions of truth change over time. Ancient religious scriptures were very concerned with protecting the reputations of elite male figures such as gods, priests, and Brahmins, but they did not have the omniscience and foresight to make sure that those elite men were presented in ways that would *always* seem appropriate! Changing social codes made old religious texts like the Bible appear *more* blasphemous than they had been to their original writers and audiences. Blasphemers suffering under the bad taste judgment in the 19th and 20th centuries were quick to point to 'beastly' and 'highly objectionable' passages in the Christian Bible which also crossed the modern decency line.

Though the idea of a decency line is deeply problematic, it has persisted in blasphemy laws worldwide. The blasphemy law in Zimbabwe protects works of a '*bona fide* literary and artistic character' from prosecution, while condemning works of a bad character. In Kuwait, a blasphemer can be punished for up to seven years, but not for speaking as one would 'in a university lecture'—that is (making it clear what is expected of a university lecturer!) in 'a calm and balanced way'. The Kuwaiti law makes explicit what is often implicit. The tone and music and pitch of the utterance have always been important in adjudications of what counts as 'blasphemy'. Laws based on the Indian penal code refer to 'uttering…any word or *making any sound*…' (my emphasis). Until they were repealed in 2018 and 2019 respectively, the laws of blasphemous libel in Canada and New Zealand used exactly the same formula about protecting criticisms of religion made 'in good faith' and 'conveyed in decent language', threatening imprisonment for one or two years for statements not made in good faith and not conveyed in decent language.

Blasphemy: a medieval crime?

The one thing that can be predicted about a chapter on blasphemy laws is that it will be out of date as soon as the pixels are dry. Even as I write, blasphemy laws are going down like ninepins—but are also being introduced, or ramped up—across the globe. The 2017 report, *Measuring the World's Blasphemy Laws*, manages to get a hasty footnote in about the repeal of the blasphemy law in Denmark (2017) (repealed just in time for a man who posted a video of himself on Facebook burning the Qur'an to escape prosecution), but still lists Canada (abolished 2018) and New Zealand (abolished 2019) among the seventy-one countries with blasphemy laws. Since the publication of the global survey, Mauritania, which upgraded blasphemy to a capital crime in 2018, has been added to the six countries (Afghanistan, Iran, Nigeria, Pakistan, Saudi Arabia, and Somalia) where blasphemy is a capital crime.

Popular accounts of blasphemy laws often imagine the crime of blasphemy as retro-religious or 'medieval', and nurture the fantasy that we are busy liberating ourselves from the hangovers of this medieval and religious past. At the repeal of the recent Irish blasphemy law, a spokesperson from Atheist Ireland announced: 'It means that we've got rid of a medieval crime from our constitution that should never have been there...' In his protest documentary *Don't Get Me Started*: *What's Wrong with Blasphemy?*, British stand-up comedian Stewart Lee quips that, though his popular musical was axed due to public accusations of blasphemy, he was not prosecuted in a court of law 'presumably on the grounds that it isn't 1508'. The thing about '1508' and 'the medieval' is that you can say what you like about them, because there is no one to speak up for them. There is no Medieval Defence League, though some medieval historians (e.g. Kathleen Biddick, Geraldine Heng, and Kathleen Davis) have written about how the 'medieval' (not unlike 'religion') can function as a contrast to the times that we live in, or hope to live in, *now*.

The rather comforting idea that moderns are fighting against a medieval crime runs aground as soon as we tune in to all the news reports on blasphemy laws worldwide. News of recent repeals of laws (the United Kingdom in 2008; the Netherlands in 2013; Iceland in 2015; Alsace in 2016) collides with reports of new blasphemy laws. The Irish blasphemy law voted out in the 2018 referendum and repealed in 2020 was controversially established in 2009. Russia passed new laws against 'offending the religious feelings of believers' in 2013, specifically in response to Pussy Riot. There are also many examples of the intensification and amplification of historical laws. Between 1947 and 1986, only fourteen cases of blasphemy were reported in Pakistan. But between 1980 and 1986, the military government of General Zia ul-Haq extended the range and severity of the blasphemy laws. In the thirty years between 1987 and 2017, 720 Muslims, 516 Ahmadi Muslims, 238 Christians, and 31 Hindus were accused of blasphemy according to the Centre for Social Justice in Pakistan.

The complex and uneven pattern of blasphemy laws worldwide upsets any illusion that the 'medieval' crime of blasphemy is gradually going the way of the dodo. There is a long *tradition* of proclaiming blasphemy dead and obsolete, but despite this, blasphemy laws have persisted in Europe and other Western countries (and some states in the USA) until the 21st century. Twenty-first-century campaigners for the abolition of blasphemy laws often cite the British judge Lord Denning who announced, back in 1949, that the offence of blasphemy was a 'dead letter'. In 1883, at the same time as the Coleridge judgment, Sir James Fitzjames Stephen confidently declared that prosecutions for blasphemy were 'theoretically possible', but in practice had become 'all but obsolete'. Hypatia Bradlaugh-Bonner (the daughter of the first atheist MP Charles Bradlaugh) captures the historical irony perfectly when she writes in *Penalties Upon Opinion* (1935): 'Yet the sheets of [Justice Stephens's] book were hardly dry from the printer's hands when a series of vindictive prosecutions for blasphemy took place.' Several of the blasphemy laws repealed in the 21st century were only established in the 20th. The blasphemy law abolished in the Netherlands in 2013 was only drafted in the 1930s, based on a relatively recent law from the 1880s. Pier Paolo Pasolini's prosecution for blasphemy in the 1960s was based on the blasphemy laws in the Fascist Rocco Code from the 1930s.

Blasphemy laws are often a symptom of political and religious insecurity. They come and go with shifts in global politics. The rise and fall of communism and fascism have played a crucial role, impacting on national blasphemy laws in different ways. The blasphemy laws used against Pasolini were passed under Mussolini in 1930. The new blasphemy law passed in the Netherlands in 1932 targeted the Communist publication, *The Tribune*. The perceived communist threat led to a doubling down on the blasphemy laws in the 1930s in England and Wales. When countries like Russia and Poland emerged from a doctrinaire secularism into a 'spiritual renaissance' in the 1990s, blasphemy laws were newly minted and augmented to reassert fundamental Christian values. The stage for Pussy Riot's blasphemy—the Cathedral of Christ the Saviour in Moscow—was destroyed by Stalin in 1931 to make way for a colossal Palace of the Soviets, which was never built. The site became a municipal swimming pool, before being rebuilt as a church in the 1990s. The public performance of state-church outrage at the blasphemies of Pussy Riot helped to *reconsecrate* the cathedral (and the nation) as a Christian space. The actions of the punk band were compared to the persecution of believers by the Bolshevik Union of the Militant Godless, who set pornographic lyrics to liturgical music, crucified priests, and put believers in psychiatric wards. There is no standard cookie-cutter history of blasphemy. National context is crucial.

How have blasphemy laws changed?

In Britain in the 17th and 18th centuries, 'blasphemers' were often subjected to spectacular and public punishments that wore their Christian/religious inspiration on their sleeve. They were publicly paraded and put on show in the pillory, lashed, whipped through the streets, 'sackclothed' (as a sign of repentance), executed, and imprisoned. Their books were burnt before their eyes by the hangman. Punishments were branded and 'stigmatized' onto their bodies. Faces were bored with B for Blasphemer, and tongues were cut or bored through with a hot iron, in a graphic punishment that took its inspiration from a passage about the dangers and powers of the tongue in the New Testament book of James. Thomas Aikenhead, the 19-year-old theology student who has the dubious honour of being the last man to be executed for blasphemy in the United Kingdom, expected to be imprisoned and 'sackclothed' but was in fact hanged on the gibbet in Edinburgh in 1697. The Quaker James Nayler was publicly 'crucified' in 1656—though some of the Parliamentarians who voted on his punishment argued that he should have been stoned.

The evolution of blasphemy laws seems to follow the pattern that the French historian of ideas, Michel Foucault, outlines in his famous book *Discipline and Punish*. Essentially, Foucault argues that as punishment became less spectacular (moving from public displays of hanging, drawing, and quartering to a carefully policed prison system), it became more effective, as people learnt to internalize discipline and censor and police themselves. Punishments for blasphemy seem to fit this paradigm. They became less visible, less spectacular, less overtly scriptural—and therefore all the more effective. Pillories and executions were abolished, but blasphemers were imprisoned with hard labour. Blasphemers no longer lost their lives. They lost their livelihoods. Offending books and newspapers were no longer publicly burnt, but were taxed and penalized out of existence. The families of imprisoned blasphemers lost any source of income and became destitute. Displays of public, ritualized vengeance on the blasphemer's body were replaced—very effectively—with social shaming and the threat of financial ruin. To protect themselves from prosecution, booksellers and customers used complex systems of dials and ropes so that they would not see one another, or be called to act as witnesses against one another. Internalizing the censorship of the law, many simply avoided 'blasphemy', while others designed ingenious workarounds for escaping prosecution.

Modern states have been able to police and prosecute blasphemy far *more* effectively than medieval or early modern societies. In his posthumously published *Open Letter*, the murdered *Charlie Hebdo* caricaturist, Charb, mocks the idea of being watched by a Big God in the Sky, imagined as 'A super-surveillance camera…installed without input from a single elected official or voter'. But pre-modern gods and societies did not have all the recording equipment and surveillance cameras possessed by highly developed modern states. The old gods might be described as omniscient, but they had nothing like the machinery of data capture and surveillance that enabled the Indian Ministry of Communications and Information Technology to enforce the new regulation in 2013 that all social media networks must remove blasphemous content within thirty-six hours of receiving a complaint. In the past, blasphemy prosecutions were local and ad hoc. Thomas Aikenhead was convicted based on the verbal testimony of his Judas-friends. Now blasphemies are on record in the public sphere, and the public sphere is undergoing constant change.

As they try to keep pace with these changes, recent blasphemy laws have started to redefine *public* blasphemies as 'Talking or shouting, whether publicly or transmitted mechanically, so that…they are…heard by those who have nothing to do with them'; 'shouting…or a deed insinuated in public, by writing, drawing, pictures/photographs, marks, and symbols, or any other method of representation made in public, or in any other means of publicness…'; '[something] declared openly or reiterated via any mechanical method at a general meeting, on a public road or at any other frequented place…or diffused by wireless or any other method' or 'displayed such that whoever is found on the public road or at any frequented place can see them'. These examples, which are taken from the Egyptian and Syrian blasphemy laws, combine old-fashioned spatial definitions of the public (on the 'public road', in the streets, the square, anywhere outside the house) with new understandings of public space transformed by radio, wi-fi, and 'mechanical methods'. They jump from older models of amplification (such as shouting in a public protest) to new technologies of amplification, such as posting messages online. Recent 'blasphemers', such as Raif Badawi in Saudi Arabia or Mohamed Cheikh Ould Mkhaïtir in Mauritania, have been prosecuted for personal blogs and Twitter posts to friends.

One of the things that legal experts often say about blasphemy is that it has been *secularized*. Whereas once it applied to the purely sacred, now it applies to the social: specifically the social understood as (a) public peace and public order and (b) the feelings of religious believers. This is true, but only to a point, and only so long as we appreciate the fact that blasphemy has always been a social crime from the start. As we saw from our brief tour of world religions, blasphemy has never been purely about the holy reputation of God or the sacred. It has also been about the protection of *dharma*, or the community embodied in the figure of Muhammad. Central to the Islamic blasphemy and apostasy laws is the idea of protecting the community from *fitnah*: chaos and civil unrest. We usually think of religious and secular laws as opposites. But the idea of blasphemy in religious laws and scriptures is very *like* the modern legal definitions of blasphemy. Both focus on the protection of institutions, communal values, and the public peace.

This is not to say that modern blasphemy laws are the same as traditional religious laws. There are at least two major differences. First, modern blasphemy laws tend to be more individualized, personalized, and focused on the feelings of religious believers. Second, they have also (but only recently, and far later than we might have imagined) moved towards protecting all religions and ideologies, including non-religious ideologies, which are often called in contemporary legal parlance 'philosophical beliefs' (to be seen as of equal value as religious beliefs).

In my own research I have argued that modern blasphemy laws have shifted the emphasis from *reverence* for God to *respect* for the believer and her/his feelings. The zone of the holy has gradually relocated to the inner life of the believer. This is now what must be protected. As a sign of this distinctly modern shift, the French law of 1819 targeted '*outrage à la morale religieuse*' (outrage to religious morality/religious insult), and the Indian Penal Code of 1927 referred to acts 'intended to *outrage religious feelings* of any class of citizens in India'. Whereas the Prussian Criminal Code of 1851 describes a blasphemer as one who 'blasphemes God or mocks one of the Christian churches...or the objects of its reverence, its teachings, institutions or customs', the updated German law of 1969 refers to the 'defamation of the religion or ideology of others in a manner that is capable of disturbing the public peace'. The old religious laws were all about protecting the established authorities: kings, gods, Brahmins—not women, slaves, or those who were already low down in the social pecking order and so could not be blasphemed. Now protection against blasphemy is often extended to all religious groups and all religious feelings, equally (or at least this is the legal aspiration). Many have argued that this has inadvertently led to a *rise* in blasphemy accusations and prosecutions, as different identity groups compete for recognition and protection in the public sphere.

The recent move to *extend* protections against blasphemy to all religious groups is in conflict with the call that has come, repeatedly, since 2011 (from the Council of Europe and the UN's 2013 Rabat Plan of Action) to abolish blasphemy laws. The problem is not just that definitions of blasphemy are 'vague', as the former UN Special Rapporteur on Religious Freedom, Heiner Bielefeldt, complains. The policy on legal retribution for religious hurt has been *conflicted*, not just unclear. Reflecting a common pattern across Europe, the repeal of the blasphemy law in Britain was timed to coincide with a new Racial and Religious Hatred Act (2006), based on the concept of hate speech. Though no one points this out, the recent reintroduction of the legal concept of words that express hate or hurt religious feelings comes strangely close to the old idea of *blasphēmía* as words or acts that cause pain. The European Court of Human Rights in Strasbourg has regularly made judgments *upholding* the protection of 'religious sensitivities'. In the most famous cases, the ECHR upheld the decision by the British Board of Film Classification to refuse a certificate to Nigel Wingrove's film *Vision of Ecstasy* and enforced the Austrian ban on Werner Schroeter's film *Liebeskonzil*. In both cases, blasphemy accusations were, once again, centred on sex. In the Wingrove case, the case against the film was upheld because of the so-called *margin of appreciation*, which allows a member state to derogate from European norms on the principle that 'the requirements of morals vary from time to time and from place to place, especially in our era…'. This is a dangerous logic in a global context where cultural exceptionalism on the grounds of a unique national 'public morality' is used to justify jailing, torturing, and executing religious dissidents in countries such as Saudi Arabia and Iran.

There is a global call to abolish blasphemy laws—and/but increased legal policing of offence to sensitivities. Legally and culturally, we seem to be undecided between two extremes. On one hand there is a tendency towards heightened self-surveillance and sensitivity. Universities issue 'trigger warnings'. A course that I used to teach at the University of Glasgow now contains a 'trigger warning' because students might be upset by scenes of crucifixion. At the same time, the widespread verdict on the massacres in Paris in 2015 is that 'blasphemy' and 'hurting religious feelings' are phantom offences that do not really exist.

The jury is out, so to speak, on the difference between hate speech and blasphemy legislation. Some argue that the British Racial and Religious Hatred Act, for example, is more precise and much safer than the old blasphemy laws, as it targets 'threatening words or behaviour' and limits the offence to those who 'intend to "stir up religious hatred"'. Others worry about the legal tests for '*intention to stir up hatred*'. A footnote to the Act makes it clear that the Act 'in no way prohibits or restricts discussion, criticism, or expressions of antipathy, dislike, ridicule, insult or abuse of particular religions or the beliefs or practices of its adherents'. But how are antipathy and abuse to be separated from threat?

In legal terms, Sikhs and Jews count as 'racial' groups, but Muslims and Christians count as 'religious' groups. Protecting groups from hurt on religious grounds is far more controversial than protecting groups from racist abuse. Many have protested that you simply cannot make religion into what European law calls a 'protected characteristic', because religion is not the same kind of thing as other protected characteristics such as disability, race, sexuality, or age. A Danish legal commentator spoke for many when, in an article on the Danish cartoon affair of 2005, he asked, 'On what grounds can you equate unchangeable race (skin colour) and religion, if religion is a matter of choice?' The idea that religion must be protected, just like race, runs head-on into one of the major modern ideas about blasphemy that we looked at in Chapter 2, 'Blasphemy in scarequotes'. As George Foote boldly argued, and Charb repeated, hurting ideas or beliefs has nothing to do with hurting real people because gods and religions are not real. However, others worry that attacks on religion ('blasphemy') are being used, by some, as an acceptable form of attack on ethnic minorities, now that racial attacks are relatively taboo.

The concepts of race and religion have very different histories in democratic societies. Modern democracies are founded on the right/freedom to criticize and attack religion. There is no parallel idea that attacking race is a foundational right—quite the opposite. Attacking people for reasons of race is widely seen as a crime that should be firmly in the past. *Opposing* the legal conflation of religion and race is now the reason given by many 'blasphemers', like Charb at *Charlie Hebdo*, as to why they feel a duty to 'blaspheme'. Ironically, new legislation to protect citizens from religious hate speech may be one reason why 'blasphemies' are on the rise.

The theatre of law

Law is often described as *theatre*. Though the concept has yet to be applied to blasphemy, some legal scholars, like Andreas Philippopoulos-Mihalopoulos, have begun to study law as an *atmosphere*, reaching far beyond the courts. Both ideas—law as theatre and law as atmosphere—are very helpful in thinking about the operation and effects of blasphemy laws.

The trial of Pussy Riot was famously described as a show trial and a media circus. The accused sat in a glass cage and protested against vague indictments for crimes of 'encroaching on [Christianity's] equality, identity and high meaningfulness', 'desiring to inflict deep spiritual wounds', or 'diminishing...the spiritual basis of the state'. The outcome was already certain because the group had already been convicted in the so-called court of public opinion by Patriarch Kirill's sermon in the church of Risopolozhenie, Moscow, where he had proclaimed, 'Every believer could not not be hurt'.

Less famously, here are the judges' words to the jury from the Gott case (where Gott was sentenced to nine months with hard labour, in 1922) and the *Gay News* Trial of 1977 (where the newspaper editor Denis Lemon was given a suspended jail sentence and a fine).

Judge addressing the jury in the trial of John William Gott, 1922:

You must put it to yourself, *supposing you received by post some abominable libel upon yourself... what is your first instinct?* Is it not the instinct of every man who is worthy of the name of a man—*the instinct is to thrash the man or*

(continued)

Continued

the woman who has written a libel on him? and that is why
the law says that it is calculated to provoke a breach of the
peace... You must ask yourself if a person of strong
religious feelings had stopped to read this pamphlet
whether his instinct might not have been to go up to the
man who was selling and give him a thrashing, or at all
events to use such language to him that a breach of the
peace might be likely to be occasioned...

Alan King-Hamilton QC addressing the jury in the *Gay News*
case, 1977:

When, therefore, ladies and gentleman, you are
considering this poem [James Kirkup's poem, 'The Love
that Dares to Speak its Name'] you must try to recapture in
your minds the impact it made upon you when you first
read it. Doubtless, the fact that you were confined in the
jury box in a court of law provided its own restraints, but
what would your reactions have been if you had first read it
or had it read aloud to you in your home, or a friend's
home, or a public house? Moreover, now, after a week you
are used to it. It is the first reaction that you must try to
recall. A medical student present at his first operation quite
frequently—not always of course, but quite frequently—
faints at the sight of blood, the shock; but after a time he
gets used to it and it does not mean anything to him. So
you must not judge it by what you think about it now; it is
your first, immediate reaction, because that is the time
when, if at all, your anger or anybody else's anger might
well be aroused or their resentment provoked...

These emotive appeals to the jury remind me of the definitions of blasphemy that we touched on at the end of Chapter 2 as 'the feeling that one gets when his [*sic*] house is broken into' or 'the righteous indignation' that wells up when 'someone touches your most serious psychological nerves'. With considerable theatrical flourish, both judges start by inviting the juries to imagine their personal feelings if a libel came into their *home* (which it hasn't: *Gay News* or Gott's *The Truthseeker* have not been posted through their letterbox). They then ask them to use their imagined anger to empathize with the strong religious feelings of others. In these judgments from 1922 and 1977, both judges *validate*—rather than criticize—the understandable instinct of individuals and communities to lash out and demand retribution. In Lord Hamilton's strong nudge to the jury, the legal theatre even turns into a metaphorical operating theatre. To help them recall/imagine their initial revulsion, the jury is invited to picture the disgust of the rookie medical student, gagging at the sight of blood.

In the case of blasphemy laws, the connection between theatre, television, and law has been particularly dramatic and not very hard to spot. The barrister representing Denis Lemon in the *Gay News* trial was none other than John Mortimer, famous for his TV role as *Rumpole of the Bailey*. Mortimer/Rumpole also acted as the legal consultant who advised the Pythons on how to dodge blasphemy prosecution during the production of *Life of Brian*. British Muslim Abdul Choudhury failed in his attempt to bring *The Satanic Verses* to trial because the British blasphemy law only protected Anglican Christians. But the case was brought to media trial on the TV show *Hypotheticals: A Satanic Scenario*, chaired by the barrister Geoffrey Robinson QC.

In the special case of blasphemy, the effects of the *atmosphere* of law are very clear. Mashal Khan (see Chapter 2) was not killed by the courts, but vigilantes inspired by Prime Minister Nawaz Sharif's crackdown on blasphemous material on social media.

10. The Trial of *Monty Python's Life of Brian*. Mervyn Stockwood (the Bishop of Southwark) and Malcolm Muggeridge, playing judge to John Cleese and Michael Palin on the popular talk show *Friday Night, Saturday Morning*, 9 November 1979.

The existence of blasphemy laws creates an atmosphere where non-legal authorities, such as museum committees or newspapers, pass judgment as if they were judges or juries in a court of law. A really interesting 'case'—that is well worth a watch—is the special edition of the BBC television show *Friday Night, Saturday Morning* where the Bishop of Southwark (Mervyn Stockwood) and Malcolm Muggeridge appeared alongside two of the writers of *The Life of Brian*, Michael Palin and John Cleese (see Figure 10). Muggeridge and the Bishop clearly imagined that they were there to act as legal and religious judges, indicting Cleese and Palin from on high for their 'foul', sinful, and 'tenth-rate' film. The public, however, roundly sided with the Pythons and their imagined trial-by-television backfired.

Chapter 5
Blasphemy and minorities

Jews and Muslims

In Chapter 2, 'Blasphemy in scarequotes', we looked at a famous essay by T. S. Eliot where he argues that Europeans and North Americans can only 'blaspheme' (in inverted commas) in the same way that parrots curse. In fact, though most people discreetly gloss over the nastier part of the essay, Eliot sees the problem as twofold: societies are becoming post-Christian or atheist, and they are becoming multicultural or multi-religious. The problem is not just the loss of belief, but the rise of beliefs, plural. For a true blasphemy, Eliot says, you need a *tradition*, which he describes as 'a way of feeling and acting which characterises a group through generations' and a sense of place 'moulded by numerous generations of one race'. In a passage that is far less parroted than the catchy little parrot phrase (and for obvious reasons), he says:

> …where two or more cultures exist in the same place they are likely either to be fiercely self-conscious or both to become adulterate. What is still more important is the unity of religious background; and *reasons of race and religion* combine to make any number of freethinking Jews undesirable. (my emphasis)

T. S. Eliot rather likes the idea that a tradition changes in time. He is far less open to the idea that different traditions, and religions/races, get mixed up in space.

Ideas about blasphemy have changed with the increasingly visible presence of religious and ethnic minorities. To clarify the concept, 'minority' is not about numbers. Women, for example, can be a 'minority' because minority refers to levels of public representation, visibility, and respect.

In Chapter 2 we looked at the *civil disabilities* imposed on religious minorities (like Jews, atheists, and nonconformist Christians), who could not pass the test for entering public office in Law or Parliament: taking holy communion according to the rites of the Anglican Church. We saw how in Britain these civil disabilities were abolished for Catholics and nonconformists in 1828; for Jews in 1858; and for public atheists in 1888. Ethnic and religious minorities did not just enter public life through immigration. Minorities who had been present for generations became newly visible as civil disabilities were lifted. Though no one has discussed this important fact, the *context* of the famous Coleridge judgment discussed in Chapter 4 was the recent removal of civil disabilities for the Jews. During George Foote's trial, Foote and Lord Coleridge had a long debate about the fact that the judge and jury could now be Jewish. They agreed that this very specific social fact meant that definitions of blasphemy as a crime against the *content* of the Christian religion no longer made any sense. Foote took the view that 'blasphemy' was therefore completely absurd. Coleridge took the view that it needed to be repurposed as a crime of manners, style, and taste.

In the pre-modern period, Jews were often the chief target for blasphemy accusations and the Talmud was regularly burnt for its 'blasphemies of Jesus and Mary' and 'foolish and revolting tales'. Modern blasphemy laws tended to limit blasphemy to a crime that could only be committed by those educated as Christians against

Christianity—with the result that Jews could not blaspheme, nor could Judaism be blasphemed against. Jews were invisible. The author of the British Home Office memo in 1913 who wrote '*if* it were shown that aspersions on the Jewish religion were regular occurrences [then] a case could be made for extending the blasphemy laws' had things backwards. Law makes groups visible and invisible. Attacks on the Jewish religion would only have become visible if there had been a blasphemy law making blasphemy against Judaism an offence.

Jews have rarely been present in modern blasphemy cases as accusers/victims or defendants. But 'Jews' have been very present as images in blasphemy controversies—and became more and more so in the modern period. Many Enlightenment thinkers and public blasphemers used what I call the 'virtual Jew' or the 'Jew hologram' to make their point. Look back at the cartoon from George Foote's blasphemous Bible cartoons: 'Moses Getting a Back View' (Figure 7). Times, tastes, and 'blasphemies' change. The Pythons never anticipated how offensive the use of blackface would become to students in 2019. Today, George Foote's cartoons appear as relatively mild blasphemies against religion—certainly when compared to contemporary Muhammad cartoons. But Foote could never have anticipated just how much social pain and anger would be provoked, now, by his portrayal of Moses as an anti-Semitic caricature.

I have deliberately chosen one of the more printable examples from Foote's Bible cartoons. The Jewish God is often presented as a cartoonish goblin, with a hook nose. Another cartoon presents a poor non-Jewish victim, like Foote, being sentenced by the harsh and vindictive *Jew Judges*. This is deeply ironic, given that Foote and his contemporaries were very well aware that Jews had only recently been able to be on juries, or serve as judges. The cartoon only makes sense in the context of Christian teaching which depicts the Jews (that is, the hologram Jews) as the 'ones-who-are-violently-sensitive-to-blasphemy' and the dogged representatives of The Law.

Why was Foote, the atheist, using the old Christian stereotypes? Like many of the campaigners for freethought, he started with familiar negative Christian stereotypes of the Old Testament and Jewishness, and then tried to get his audience to apply them to the whole Christian tradition, which, he argued, now had no more value than the religion of 'Mumbo-Jumbo' or the 'tribal God of the Jews'. Though he was a public atheist, using blasphemy to create legitimate space for the new (minority) movement known as secularism or atheism, Foote automatically repeated the Christian caricature of the Jews as the representatives of unmerciful and vengeful law. This was a very common move. In his trial in 1844 (the last trial for blasphemy in Scotland), Edinburgh bookseller Thomas Paterson compared himself to Jesus and his persecutors to the Jews, that 'savagely intolerant race' who believed that it was their duty 'to kill every soul that breathed what they considered blasphemy'. Though Jews could not act as judges, or bring a case of blasphemy, the draconian prosecutors for blasphemy were regularly associated with 'the Jews', modelled on the Jews in the Gospel story of Jesus's trial.

Since the late 1970s and 1980s (much later than we might expect), the majority position on blasphemy in Europe and the Nordic countries has turned through 180 degrees. In the past, the moral majority was *against* blasphemy and the blasphemer was the outsider, the threat. Now the normative position is to see tolerating or even celebrating blasphemy as one of the definitions of modern Western democracies, and even the condition of newcomers being admitted to modern democracies. There is still more than a little of 'the past' in the 'now' (as we can see from our survey of global blasphemy laws in Chapter 4). But whereas in the past Western states prosecuted or condemned blasphemy, today tolerating blasphemy is widely regarded as an essential element in the definition of Western democratic tradition. The thing about tradition, as T. S. Eliot notes, is that it is versatile and can easily be revised.

As the opposition to blasphemy has become, gradually, a minority position, the opposition to blasphemy has been associated with minorities: first with Jews; then with Muslims. Today it is very common for blasphemy to be represented as a Muslim problem. But this has only been the case in the period that we could call ASV, or 'After the *Satanic Verses* Affair' of 1989. In the period BSV (Before *The Satanic Verses*), references to Islam are minimal and tend to use comparisons with Muhammad as a way of commenting on Christianity and Christ. One of the blasphemies of Thomas Woolston (1668–1733) was to have said that if the miracles ascribed to Jesus had been recorded of 'Mahomet', then the Christian theologians would have been quick to condemn him as 'nothing less than a Wizard, an Enchanter, a Dealer with familiar spirits, a sworn Slave to the devil'. One of the incendiary remarks that sent Thomas Aikenhead to the gallows in 1697 was comparing Christ unfavourably to Moses and Muhammad, saying that Moses was the better artist and the better politician and that he preferred Muhammad to Christ.

The first modern 'blasphemous' cartoon of Muhammad

The first accidentally 'blasphemous' Muhammad cartoon in modern Europe was drawn by the famous British cartoonist David Low, and was actually about cricket. Drawn in 1925, the cartoon 'It' was a celebration of the star cricketer Jack Hobbs, who the day before had scored his 126th century and become 'It'. 'Mahomet' was one of the mini figures in a comic Gallery of the Most Important Historical Celebrities (alongside Adam, Julius Caesar, Charlie Chaplin, Christopher Columbus, and David Lloyd George, the then Prime Minister) who were dwarfed by the cricketing giant.

In his autobiography, Low explains that, having been ticked off by his editor for comic use of Christian imagery in a previous cartoon, he chose Muhammad to avoid the far more controversial figure of Christ. In a newspaper with a large circulation (and *The Star* was selling 700,000 copies a day) there were, he said, 'always too many toes to tread on'. He chose Muhammad because he had far fewer 'toes' under him than Jesus. He selected Muhammad in order to *avoid* giving offence. Fast forward to the second decade of the 21st century, and the publisher of this book has taken the decision to omit the cartoon so as not to cause offence.

Low imagined no (or very few) Muslim toes in Britain in the 1920s. So he and his editor were taken aback by the pushback from the small but growing Ahmadi Muslim community in Britain—the same group now targeted by the updated colonial blasphemy laws in Pakistan. A letter was sent to Low's newspaper and protests circulated in India. We only know this from the account in Low's autobiography, where he describes a poster in India asking Muslims to 'give unmistakable proof of their love of Islam by asking the Government of India to compel the British Government to submit the editor of the newspaper in question to such an ear-twisting that it may be an object-lesson to other newspapers'. Low then adds, with a wink, 'The British Government was unresponsive, for we heard no more', and comments, 'It is not without a twinge of regret that I reflect upon the loss to history of a picturesque scene on Tower Hill, with plenty of troops, policemen and drums, on the occasion of my unfortunate editor having his ears twisted on my behalf.'

David Low's mockery of the Muslim protest seems condescending and colonial. Though by no means a pious Christian, he automatically repeats the cartoonish caricatures of other religions, representing Islam as dangerous, zealous—but also ineffective, powerless, and rather quaint. The comic image of a Muslim-led prosecution for blasphemy on Tower Hill shows how far Low and his contemporaries imagine Muslims to be from the symbolic centres of power. By imagining a retro-medieval prosecution at the Tower of London, Low also seems to assume (just three years after the imprisonment of John William Gott in 1922) that in modern Britain punishments for blasphemy are a blast from the medieval past.

The *Satanic Verses* Affair

When Salman Rushdie's novel *The Satanic Verses* was first published in 1988, I was a second-year undergraduate reading English Literature. Now when I teach what became known as 'the *Satanic Verses* Affair', I start by introducing students who are accustomed to a very different tone in the public discussion of race and religion to the foreign country of the 1980s. I introduce these sometimes shocked migrants to a world were everyday racism was naturalized in sitcoms such as *Love thy Neighbour*, *Mind your Language*, and *It Ain't Half Hot Mum*. Together we read Rushdie's essay 'The New Empire within Britain' (1982), and look at the litany of racist statements from the political establishment, the judiciary, the police, as well as the National Front. One of Rushdie's examples is Lord Denning, whom we already met in Chapter 4. Like T. S. Eliot, Lord Denning regularly gets into introductions to blasphemy with his famous pronouncement from 1949 that blasphemy is a 'dead letter' (discussed in Chapter 4). Rushdie cites another, less congenial, statement from Lord Denning: black and brown citizens should not sit on juries because they do not 'share the same standards of conduct'. Like T. S. Eliot, Denning is very anxious about the fact that the English are no longer a 'homogeneous race'.

Today some universities have programmes on decolonizing the curriculum and challenging norms of whiteness. Back in the 1980s, studying on what was then a fairly canonical English Literature degree, *The Satanic Verses* was the first novel to set me thinking about migration and moving between worlds. I was powerfully affected by this story of 'two brown men', Gibreel Farishta and Saladin Chamcha, magically crashing into London, known in the novel as *Vilayet* (the Hindi term for 'foreign place') or Margaret Thatcher's Ellowen Deeowen. Gibreel and Saladin are spat upon by racists and imprisoned as 'illegal' immigrants. But they also undergo fabulous metamorphoses as, in audacious acts of 'blasphemy' (Rushdie's own word), they take on the creator's role and re-create themselves as mutant mobile creatures made up of 'bits and fragments from here, there'.

Looking through my old copy of the novel I see that I have marked lines such as: 'Question: what is the opposite of faith? Not disbelief. Too final, certain, closed. Itself a kind of belief. Doubt' and 'What kind of idea are you?...Are you the kind that compromises, does deals, accommodates itself to society, aims to find a niche, to survive; or are you the cussed, bloody-minded, ramrod-backed type of damnfool notion that would rather break than sway with the breeze?—The kind that will almost certainly, ninety-nine times out of hundred, be smashed to bits; but, the hundredth time, will change the world.' With very little religious literacy beyond my 'home' religion, Christianity, I thought of Salman Rushdie rather like William Blake. I did not know that the title *The Satanic Verses* was a specific allusion to a disputed tradition about what Muhammad said about the three goddesses, Al-Lat, Al-Uzza, and Manat, who were worshipped in pre-Islamic times.

The tradition of the satanic verses is another example of the pre-modern fluidity in religious traditions that we discussed in Chapter 3. In the Qur'an (Q 53.23), Muhammad makes the non-controversial statement, 'They [the goddesses] are nothing but names which you and your fathers have made up. God sent down no authority upon them': a statement consistent with pure monotheism. But al-Tabari, a 10th-century collector of stories about Muhammad's life, tells a more ambiguous story: 'Satan Casts a False Revelation on the Messenger of God's Tongue'. According to al-Tabari, in order to act as a good ambassador and start a conversation with the Arab polytheists, Muhammad spoke words that seemed to accept Al-Lat, Al-Uzza, and Manat not as goddesses, but three angelic intercessionaries. However, this was a moment of temptation by the devil and Muhammad then rejected and struck out these words. Al-Tabari glosses the lesson of this episode as 'Satan casts words into Muhammad's recitation' but 'God overcomes'.

Genre is very important in the study of blasphemy. *The Satanic Verses* is a *novel*, a work of magic-realist fiction. Salman Rushdie takes the suggestive 'what if' in the concept of the satanic verses and sets it loose in fiction. *What if* a man called Mahound (the offensive slang name for Muhammad used by the Christian Crusaders) had a diabolic scribe called, let's say, Salman, who started to tweak the words dictated by Mahound, starting very modestly, almost imperceptibly, by hearing 'all-seeing, all knowing' but writing 'all knowing, all-wise'? What if he then started to get a little wilder, inspired by this idea of misfit words cast into the true recitation? What if, to focus on the parts of the novel that were seen as most offensive, he changed the word Mecca into Jahilia (the pre-Islamic city of ignorance), and imagined prostitutes calling themselves by the names of Muhammad's wives?

Though they are often misleadingly batched together as cases of 'blasphemy', *The Satanic Verses* is a very different kind of 'blasphemy' to the inner-Christian British 'blasphemies' of, say, *Monty Python's Life of Brian*. For Rushdie, making a mixed-up version of Islam was one way of exploring the 'immeasurable distance from Indianness to Englishness', and the distance between British Christian secularism and the minimal Islam of Rushdie's own childhood in Mumbai. The author protested that Mahound is not Muhammad, any more than Brian is Jesus, or the Christ figure in Martin Scorcese's film of Nikos Kazantzakis's *The Last Temptation of Christ* is the Christ of the Gospels. But the comparisons with Christ only go so far. The Pythons' *Brian* made domestic in-jokes against the British church and state. *The Satanic Verses* ran the immense risk of taking up the 'demon-tag' of the name Mahound used by the 'farangis [Europeans]' as an example of 'turn[ing] insults into strengths', just as 'whigs, tories, blacks, all chose to wear with pride the names they were given in scorn'. In the complex social ecology of awkwardly post-imperial Britain, using an abusive term for Muhammad was a risk that spectacularly backfired.

What soon became known as the '*Satanic Verses* Affair' spiralled into a 'blasphemy' far beyond anyone's intention or control. Writing in *The Guardian* in 1989, the representative of the Bradford Council of Mosques, Shabbir Aktar, declared that 'Anyone who fails to be offended by Rushdie's book *ipso facto* ceases to be a Muslim…' (just like Patriarch Kirill declaring that 'any believer could not not be hurt' by the performance by Pussy Riot). On Valentine's Day 1989, the Ayatollah Khomenei issued the famous fatwa calling for the death of Rushdie. The Ayatollah may also have been enraged by chapter IV of *The Satanic Verses*, an unflattering tale of an Imam who seems to be the spitting image of himself. (As we have seen, it is often hard to tell political and religious offence apart.)

One of the effects of the *Satanic Verses* Affair was to change the popular understanding of the word *fatwa*—which simply means 'religious edicts applying religious law to a particular situation'—into a word automatically associated with violent punishments and death sentences. Highly respected postcolonial authors such as Naghuib Mahfouz and Edward Said did not defend the author's right to freedom of expression, but condemned Rushdie for (in Said's words) not 'defending and sympathetically interpreting us' but 'representing us so roughly…and so disrespectfully to an audience already primed to excoriate our tradition, reality, history, religion, language and origins'.

This idea—that a member of a minority has a special obligation to represent that minority in a positive light—has surfaced several times in recent blasphemy controversies. When the play *Behzti*

('Dishonour') was cancelled by the Birmingham Rep in 2004 in response to mass protests by the Sikh community, the prize-winning playwright Gurpreet Kaur Bhatti was accused of having defaced the Sikh community by presenting the community with an ugly face. Just like the so-called British kitchen sink dramas of the 1960s, *Behzti* presented the drab and sordid realities behind closed doors and shone the spotlight on sexual abuse. Like Rushdie, but far less famously, Gurpreet Kaur Bhatti was assigned police protection, and had to leave her home to escape death threats.

Ironically, given Rushdie's trenchant attacks on the whiteness of the British establishment, the protest against *The Satanic Verses* was one of the first major religious-racial protests from British Muslim communities. Marching against the novel became a symbol of marching for visibility and respect. During the mass protests in Bradford and London, Muslim protesters were confronted by members of the National Front, taunting them as 'Pakis'.

Memories of these marches are often simplified. It is easy to forget the Muslims who did not support the ban and certainly did not support the fatwa, or the Muslims who tried to bring a blasphemy prosecution in the law courts, but were unable to, because they had no more legal power than the Christian Alexamenos, who had no power to protest against the representation of Jesus as donkey, however he might have felt about it (see Chapter 1). We should also restore to cultural memory the many women from groups such as Women Against Fundamentalism and Southall Black Sisters who bravely marched in support of Rushdie and were targeted from both sides, by Muslim men and the National Front.

Since this is a chapter about minority, we should pause for a moment to think about blasphemy and gender. Because, as we explored in Chapter 3, blasphemy is a *social* crime against those with the highest levels of public respect, it has tended to be a crime against the highest men: kings, Brahmins, or the men who embody the political and religious legacies of Muhammad. Until recently, blasphemies have taken the form of public attacks on male religious figures and authorities by other men. But historians are beginning to recover the stories of women who were also involved in blasphemy controversies: the female preachers and supporters of polygamy who were also targeted by the 1650 blasphemy law passed by Oliver Cromwell's Parliament (Chapter 3); the Quaker women—Martha Symonds, Hannah Stranger, and Dorcas Erbury—who were part of James Nayler's 'blasphemous' performances in Bristol; the female campaigners and lecturers on the freethought and abolition lecture circuit (like Annie Besant, or Francis Wright, or Eliza Sharples); and the wives and families who were activists alongside their husbands, like Richard Carlile's wife, Jane Carlile. As we explored in Chapter 2, although women have not been at the forefront of blasphemy controversies, women's bodies have. In the 19th and 20th centuries, blasphemy controversies were often mixed up with campaigns for what we now call birth control. Protesters against *The Satanic Verses* often concentrated on the section where prostitutes take the names of Muhammad's wives, and saw themselves as defending the honour of Muhammad's wives.

Since the 1980s, women have been returning to a more public role in blasphemy controversies and freedom of speech campaigns. The activist group Women Against Fundamentalism sees the campaign for freedom of expression as central to feminist and anti-racist agendas. Members of the feminist group Femen often protest topless to attack symbols of religious authority, arguing that the ultimate 'blasphemy' in traditional religion is the naked female body. Gurpreet Kaur Bhatti's 'blasphemous' play *Behzti* ('Dishonour') shines the spotlight on the abuse of women and girls. Borrowing images from the Iranian American video artist Shirin Neshat, the former Somalian refugee Aayan Hirsi Ali collaborated with the Dutch film-maker Theo van Gogh to make the film *Submission*, where naked women's bodies are inscribed with verses from the Qur'an. Pussy Riot deliberately staged their performance on the *ambon*—the holy altar forbidden to women—and used their lyrics to subvert conventions of gender and social respect. They pointedly addressed Patriarch Kirill as a 'bitch' (*suka*)—not, as often mistranslated, a 'bastard'. The idea here is that the worst thing that you can do to a man in contemporary society is to call him a woman. The mockery and trivialization of the band members show how social and legal judgments against female blasphemers often take a very different tone. With masculinist bravado, Vladimir Putin bragged that he had 'socked them with a twosie' by sentencing them to two years in a penal colony. A left-wing sympathizer disagreed, saying that the girls should not be imprisoned—only spanked.

The reaction to *The Satanic Verses* was chaotic and complex. Representatives of the British establishment lectured the Muslim community on the good British tradition of freedom of expression, but also condemned Rushdie. There was little sympathy with outraged Muslims. Public burnings of the book and effigies of Rushdie backfired, combining with the fatwa to reinforce caricatures of Islam as fundamentalist, violent, and 'medieval'. Many commentators started to take the opportunity to make ill-informed statements about the different essences of Christianity and Islam. For example, without referencing chapter and verse, the feminist author Fay Weldon proclaimed that whereas the Bible provides 'food for thought' out of which you can 'build a decent society', the Qur'an, in contrast, is definitely not 'a poem on which society can be safely or sensibly based' for it 'forbids change, interpretation, self-knowledge, even art, for fear of treading on Allah's creative toes'.

Protests and positions around *The Satanic Verses* ricocheted in all directions. Public memory conveniently simplified these, making the event easier to process and understand. First the affair became an Affair: a term that harks back to the Dreyfus Affair

(1894–1906) in France. By using the term applied to the trial of a Jewish officer in Europe, the case of *The Satanic Verses* was framed as a new showdown between Europe and minorities. The range of positions was simplified to just two, fuelling the agenda of those on both sides who wanted people to think in terms of easy choices between 'Islam' and 'the West'.

The Rushdie Affair broke out just before the Berlin wall came down, signalling the end of the Cold War, and just one year before Samuel Huntington published his infamous thesis on a new clash of civilizations. According to Huntington, the old cold war between the West and Soviet east had been succeeded by a new religious conflict between the Christian West and the Islamic east that was 'far more fundamental' than differences between political ideologies. This led to the transformation of ethnic difference into religious difference. In the 1980s, the era of 'Paki-bashing', minorities were caricatured according to their country of origin or the colour of their skin. In *From Fatwa to Jihad*, the writer and broadcaster Kenan Malik, from the same generation as Rushdie, recalls how he and his contemporaries identified as black rather than Muslim, Hindu, Sikh (or even Asian) back in 1988.

'I thought religion was dead and gone,' says one of the interviewees in a documentary reflecting back on the *Satanic Verses* Affair, thirty years later. Since the 1980s many have spoken about the shock of what is often called the *return of religion* (meaning the return of religion as a danger and a problem). Similarly, many have commented on the surprising return of blasphemy when we might have expected blasphemy to become extinct. The return of religion and the persistence, or return, of blasphemy are connected. Every time a controversy is labelled as 'blasphemy' it becomes another public problem of religion rather than, say, politics or race. Blasphemy was given a new lease of life as it took on a new form: the trial of minorities in the West. This started at just the same moment that Europe and Scandinavia first started to say that their national traditions had always been supportive and tolerant of blasphemy, all along.

The Danish Cartoon Affair

After Rushdie, blasphemy went relatively quiet in the 1990s, then burst back into the spotlight post-9/11 with a rebooting of the Huntington thesis and another 'affair': the Danish cartoon affair of 2005/6. The affair began when Flemming Rose, an editor at the local paper *Jyllands-Posten* in Aarhus, sent out invitations to forty-two Danish cartoonists to draw the Prophet Muhammad 'as they see him'. This was a very local affair, in the beginning. *Jyllands-Posten* had a circulation of 150,000, just one-fifth of David Low's *The Star*. The invitation was inspired by a rumour that a children's author, Kare Bluitgen, had been unable to find an illustrator for a children's book about the prophet Muhammad. The idea was to take what was widely understood as the Muslim prohibition against representing Muhammad's face (see Chapter 3) and perform the Danish commitment to freedom of speech by inviting non-Muslims to draw Muhammad's face.

Only fifteen responded and twelve agreed to publish cartoons in a special edition *Muhammeds Ansigt* ('The Face of Muhammad') on 30 September 2005. The most famous cartoon, which soon became the logo of the affair, was Kurt Westergaard's cartoon of Muhammad with a bomb in his turban. Less widely circulated was the critical cartoon by Lars Refn (see Figure 11), in which a seventh-grade boy in a school in an immigrant district of Copenhagen is writing on the blackboard, in Farsi, 'The *Jyllands-Posten* journalists are a bunch of reactionary provocateurs.'

David Low's 'blasphemous' Muhammad was entirely accidental. His aim was very simply to celebrate a cricketer's success while avoiding stepping on Christian toes. In contrast, a journalist at *Jyllands-Posten* described the Muhammad cartoon project as

Mohammed
Valbyskole 7.A

11. Cartoonist Lars Refn's contribution to 'The Face of Muhammad' special edition of *Jyllands-Posten*. Refn was criticized by religious groups but also by freedom of speech activists who attacked him for not drawing the face of Muhammad.

deliberate 'democratic electroshock therapy' for Danish Muslims. Flemming Rose declared that in democratic societies 'you must be ready to put up with insults, mockery and ridicule'. The editor-in-chief, Carsten Juste (who later issued an apology), originally said that they had published the cartoons to oppose the 'mad mullahs' who have a 'sickly sensitivity to criticism' and who are voices from the 'dark and violent middle ages'. (There goes the stigmatized 'medieval' again.)

Blasphemy returned (with a vengeance) when it was repurposed as a trial of the presumed incompatibility between Islam in general and the democratic West. Blasphemy did not die in

Europe, Scandinavia, and North America because it was used to test and produce the kinds of distinctions between Islam and the West popularized by the Huntington thesis and the *Satanic Verses* Affair. Back in 1925, when Low drew his cartoon, no one would have thought that 'mocking and insulting religious people is part of the European canon of basic values' (as Jytte Klausen puts it in her book, *The Cartoons that Shook the World*). Blasphemy was increasingly understood as a trial of religious minorities. By not reacting against the most provocative representations of their religion, communities could demonstrate their compatibility with 'the West'.

This was a high entrance bar, given that anyone who acted violently—for example, the second-generation Moroccan-Dutchman Mohammed Bouyeri, who murdered the Dutch film-maker Theo van Gogh for making the film *Submission* with Aayan Hirsi Ali—would be presented as a representative of Islam. Aware of this fact, many Muslims felt that they could not join the *Je Suis Charlie* campaign after the *Charlie Hebdo* murders in Paris, while others felt a need (not felt by Christians) to show that Islam was a religion of peace. One handwritten note at the Place de la République proclaimed: 'I swear on the holy Qur'an, that a muslim who kills in the name of Allah, blessed be his name, shall be thrown into eternal damnation.' Another said simply, 'I am a Muslim. Peace.'

Though we use the same word to describe it, suggesting continuity, blasphemy has changed considerably since the 1980s. The spotlight and the judgment are now on the one-who-is-sensitive-to-blasphemy rather than the blasphemer. To blaspheme is now seen as normative, but this has only been the case since the 1980s. Whereas the outsider was once the blasphemer, now the outsider is the one-who-is-sensitive-to-blasphemy.

Until the mid-20th century, the photofit of the deliberate blasphemer was a leftist/socialist/anarchist freethinker, campaigning for the rights of the working classes to criticize religious and political authorities, in many cases linking the case for freedom of thought to (relative) sexual freedom and birth control. Ethnicity and multiculturalism were not major issues—though, as we saw in Chapter 2, Abner Kneeland was an interesting exception, prosecuted for blasphemies of class, sex, and *race*. Today the photofit of the deliberate blasphemer is often someone who presents him/herself as a defender of what are often presented as centuries-old (?) European and American values of freedom of speech, against immigrant communities who are not accustomed to freedom of speech, and also sexual freedom (the limitation of which is now often firmly associated with Islam). The idea of blasphemy is now dominated by (a) cartoons of Muhammad and (b) burnt or abused Qur'ans.

Whereas the majority of activist 'blasphemers' used to be from the political left, now they are sometimes from the left, but also from the right. Figures such as Bat-Ye'or, Geert Wilders, Thilo Sarrazin, Niall Ferguson, and his wife Aayan Hirsi Ali link their campaign for freedom of speech to what they describe as the threat of 'Eurabia' and the takeover of the West by Muslims. In some cases, maximal provocation is clearly being used to provoke a violent reaction from at least one 'Muslim', thus setting up a feedback loop that bolsters the public image of blasphemy-sensitive and intolerant Islam. In 2008, the right-wing Dutch parliamentarian Geert Wilders made a short film claiming that *fitnah* (civil unrest) is *caused* by the Qur'an. It is hard to imagine a more incendiary attack on the fundamental precepts of Islam. In Denmark, the right-wing politician Rasmus Paludan fairly comprehensively desecrated a copy of the Qur'an by putting bacon between the pages, throwing it into the air and letting it fall, and dousing it in what he said was the 'semen of Christian men and non-believers', before setting it on fire.

These actions seem very different from the bold campaigns by Raif Badawi or Ashraf Fayadh or Mashal Khan, to speak out against political/religious authorities in the name of freedom in

Saudi Arabia or Pakistan. To examine why, we have to return to some of the ideas that we have already looked at: *parrhēsía*; the deep historical connection between religion and the state (blasphemy as a crime of *lèse-majesté*); and blasphemy as a crime against community order and stability, whatever name that goes by, be it *dharma* or the 'secular' public peace. Throughout history, blasphemy has been used to describe an offence by a minority against a majority and attacks on the home authorities, political and religious. Now the idea often seems to be that *we*, the home majority, should blaspheme against the holy things that have never been our holy things and that we have never cared about, in order to teach *them* (the minorities) the old Western arts of blasphemy and critique.

All this doesn't ring quite true, given the history of blasphemy and Christianity, which often gets hastily overwritten. It can also seem condescending and colonial. As one of my Muslim students put it, 'Why can they draw ugly pictures of Muhammad, when it is forbidden to me?' The stereotype of the Jew and then the Muslim (not the Christian) as the 'one-who-is-sensitive-to-blasphemy' seems to carry over stereotypes from Christian history into the campaign for freedom from religion. Often Christianity ends up on the side of the good, relatively blasphemy-tolerant religion—despite the testimony of history.

Chapter 6
Blasphemy and media

Throughout this *Very Short Introduction*, we have been exploring significant changes in blasphemy: for example, the 180-degree turn from the *condemnation* of blasphemy to the idea that freedom to blaspheme *defines* free societies; and the shift from 'blasphemous' activism by left-wing revolutionary and radical groups to 'blasphemy' led from the political right (see Chapter 5). In this final chapter, we will look at how blasphemy has been profoundly changed (but not always in the ways that we might imagine) by media revolutions: first, print, woodcuts, pamphlets, and newspapers; then, in a massive wave of transformation from the late 19th century, telegraph, radio, photography, film, and television; and finally, the age of digital technology and social media. We touched on some of these issues in Chapter 4, when we looked at how recent blasphemy laws introduced awkward phrases such as 'diffusion by wireless or any other method' or 'mechanical transmission' to reflect how new media had changed the shape of the 'public sphere'.

We begin with the turn to figures, faces, and cartoons.

The figural/facial turn

Until the 1880s, blasphemies were verbal: literally *words* that hurt. From the 1880s, blasphemy took a visual turn towards the representation of the *bodies* and *faces* of sacred figures. A new medium began to be used for blasphemy: cartoons. The association between blasphemy and cartoons did not burst out of the blue with the Danish cartoon affair or *Charlie Hebdo*. I want to (for the first time) compare these recent Muhammad cartoons to the deeply controversial Bible cartoons that sent George Foote to prison in the 1880s. We have already spent some time looking at one of these cartoons: 'Moses Getting a Back View' (Figure 7 discussed in Chapters 3 and 5).

Many of Foote's Comic Bible Sketches were based on the 401 cartoons published in the ex-Jesuit Léo Taxil's *La Bible amusante* (Comic Bible) in Paris in 1881, just after the French crime of 'outrage to religious morality' was abolished with a new law on freedom of the press. Bible cartoons were still (legally) 'blasphemous' in England and the Netherlands, where Taxil's Bible was banned. Foote took great delight in importing his illegal cartoon contraband across the Channel. He saw the deployment of cartoons as a deliberate strategy. 'Lazy minds' numbed by the 'reverence of prejudice' could easily read without feeling anything. But no one could escape the instant shock of 'pictorial ridicule', he declared.

Foote enjoyed imagining the effect of his cartoons on the ones-who-are-sensitive-to-blasphemy: in this case, the 'pious and chaste British public'. Calling on the stereotypes of Bumble (the petty bureaucrat in Dickens's *Oliver Twist*) and 'Mrs Grundy' (the personification of priggishness and conventional propriety), he announced: 'We in England have Comic Histories, Comic Geographies, and Comic Grammars, but a Comic Bible would horrify us. At the sight of such blasphemy Bumble would stand aghast, and Mrs Grundy would scream with terror.' In Foote's imagination, the sober British majority turned into a collective caricature, running away from racy French cartoons with 'shrieks of pious wrath'.

In fact, Foote often avoided racier cartoons of naked bodies and sex in the French original. The Comic Bible Sketches are also extremely tame when compared to some of the post-1980s Muhammad cartoons. The appearance of God in chequered trousers in 'Moses Getting a Back View' is almost ludicrously mild compared to the cartoons in *Charlie Hebdo*, where (for example), a grotesque cartoon Muhammad exposes his buttocks to the cameras, and Muslim women are exhorted to 'wear the burkha on the inside'.

The cartoon Bibles of the 1880s invented a new way of creating special effects of 'blasphemy': playing with anachronism, and allowing new media and technologies to intrude on ancient biblical times. Adam in the Garden of Eden reads a newspaper called *The Universe*. God's prophets are shocked (as well they might be!) to get a call on the telephone, which has only just been invented in the 1880s. Abraham takes a rifle rather than a knife to his son, and accidentally shoots God (so causing an accidental death of God) when the angel grabs the gun from his hand. Salman Rushdie plays similar media tricks in *The Satanic Verses*. One of the two main characters, Gibreel Farishta, is a Muslim who plays Hindu gods in the popular Indian films known as the theologicals. (PK, the film alien discussed at the end of Chapter 3, chases one of these 'gods' into the public toilets in his attempt to crack the mysteries of religion on earth.) Playing with the 'blasphemous' special effects of cinema, Rushdie turns Gibreel into a divinized celebrity 'between the mortal and the divine'. When posters of Gibreel's divine-celebrity face tear and fade after he has left India for Britain, Rushdie quips that his departure had led to an accidental defacing, and death, of 'god'.

In his posthumously published *Open Letter*, *Charlie Hebdo* caricaturist Charb argues that 'sticking a clown nose on Marx is no more offensive or scandalous than popping the same schnoz on Muhammad'—and vice versa. This is an argument that could only have been made relatively recently. There has been no open licence to caricature the holy figures of Christianity, and the highest and holiest political figures, such as the royal family, have often also been protected, which is why Charb is wise to select the example of Marx. In a famous case in France that we touched on in Chapter 2, Charles Philipon was fined and imprisoned for the crime of 'contempt of the king's person' for publishing pictures of King Louis Philippe of France as a pear-head in the newspaper *La Caricature* in 1831. The British government protected the royal family from visual defamation using more subtle methods: bribes and taxation on the radical press. Today, in Thailand, acts deemed insulting to the king, including media crimes (such as placing photographs of anybody on a website above photographs of the king), incur longer prison sentences than acts of blasphemy against the Buddha. In the same year as the Danish cartoon controversy, a book on the Thai monarchy with the title *The King Never Smiles* was banned by the Thai Information and Communications Ministry on the grounds that the 'contents...could affect national security and the good morality of the people'. Courageous cartoonists such as Ramón Esono Ebalé in Equatorial Guinea, Atena Farghadan in Iran, Firas Bachi in Syria, and Zunar Zulkiflee Anwar Ulhaque in Malaysia, are among the many visual artists currently in prison for caricatures of political authorities. (Compare the discussion of secular blasphemies in Chapter 2.)

Reformation woodcuts of pope-donkeys and people farting in the face of the Pope (Figure 9) can be seen as early precursors of blasphemous cartoons disfiguring religious figures—but they only deface popes, monks, and religious authorities, not sacred figures like the Virgin Mary or Jesus. Disfigurements of the beautiful, holy, bodies of Jesus and Mary were largely unthinkable, un-drawable (though early modern historian Justin Champion pointed me to the remarkable exception of Wenceslaus Hollar's *Satirical Passion* [1642–54], which he describes as a 17th-century *Life of Brian*). Until the late 19th century, negative cartoons of Jesus tended to be verbal cartoons, like Thomas Woolston's presentation of Jesus cursing the fig tree like a bad-tempered man throwing chairs about the house, or getting so drunk at the wedding in Cana that he could not recognize his own mum (see Chapter 4). All the excellent collections of blasphemous art, such as Brent Plate's *Blasphemy: Art that Offends* or the catalogue from the exhibition *Traces du sacré* (Traces of the Sacred) at the Pompidou in Paris, showcase an explosion of 'blasphemous' art from the 20th and 21st centuries. Before high art began to get really creative with the Christian tradition in works such as Paul Gauguin's *Self-Portrait with the Yellow Christ* (1890) or Max Ernst's *The Virgin Spanking the Christ Child in the Presence of Witnesses* (1926), Taxil, Foote, and other blasphemers started a revolution from below in the form of popular cartoons.

Protestant semiotic ideology: bodies versus ideas

In Chapter 2, we looked at how 'blasphemers' like George Foote led the way in distinguishing 'real persons' from mere 'ideas'. Foote was one of the first to make the argument, now regularly repeated by caricaturists like Charb, that blasphemy cannot hurt any-body, because gods and sacred figures are not real: they do not have bodies; they are only pictures, images, or ideas—or, as Foote also said, 'ghosts', traces of old beliefs. The striking fact is that this separation came at exactly the same time that Foote was introducing a new form of blasphemy based on defacing holy faces and disfiguring holy figures. At the same time that blasphemers started saying that blasphemy never hurts any-body, blasphemy started to zone in on faces and bodies, as if to prove the point.

These new visual blasphemies were very different from older models of blasphemy based on the discussion of theological ideas. As we discussed in Chapter 1, the second half of the word blasphemy comes from Greek *phēmē* , and *phēmē* has two meanings: (1) speech and (2) fame/reputation (like Latin *fama*). In the visual, figural, and facial turn, blasphemy, which was once about words (sense 1), is transformed into de-facing, dis-figuring, and shaming sacred figures (sense 2).

Defenders of European and North American cartoons of Muhammad often make the point that these are only pictures, drawing a strong distinction between a mere picture and the real thing. Anthropologist Webb Keane has described this firm division between the idea/picture/sign and the real thing as 'Protestant semiotic ideology'. In Protestant tradition, the bread and wine are not the real body and blood of Christ. They are only signs, representations. There is a broken circuit—or gap—between the real thing and the sign (or picture or idea).

But this separation is not as clear as it might seem. Saba Mahmood has argued that Protestant semiotic ideology can hardly be applied to all cultures, as if everyone were Protestant or Christian. Art theorist W. J. T. Mitchell and cultural theorist Sigrid Weigel have made the important point that this division between ideas/pictures and the real thing is not at all consistent, even in Protestant and post-Protestant countries. Instead there is a *double relation* to images and pictures. Pictures are treated as if they are nothing, nothing real—and/but they are *also* described as if they have incredible, even magical, power.

In this age of the selfie, when so many young people and celebrities are involved in such obsessive tending of their public faces, the idea that a disfigured image may cause pain to a real person should not seem so very strange. When his students doubt their own cultural belief in the power of images, W. J. T. Mitchell shows them that they do not really believe that 'pictures are just pictures' by asking them to cut holes through the eyes of a photograph of their mum.

Sigrid Weigel argues that modern blasphemous cartoons revive older traditions of defacing and defaming a person using drawings

12. Defamation: the Severan Tondo (*c.*199 CE), with one of the son's faces wiped out.

of the face/figure as proxy. The Alexamenos graffito in Rome (*c.*200 CE) extends the social humiliation of the crucifixion in the form of a cartoon (cf. Chapter 1). In the Roman tradition of *Damnatio memoriae*, faces of offending figures were blanked out—not as a gesture of respect, which is sometimes the case with pictures of Muhammad—but quite the reverse (see Figure 12).

In the Italian and German 'shame pictures' from 1400 to 1600 (known as *pittura infamante* and *Schandbilder*), debtors and breakers of contracts were hung upside down, flagellated by the devil, or cut up into pieces—but not in person, only on paper and ink (Figure 13). Those convicted of bad speech were given shame

13. Humiliated figure hung upside down and whipped by a devil. German *Schandbild*, or 'shame picture', *c*.1460.

masks, which turned them into a walking caricature or cartoon (Figure 14). Like Reformation and Counter-Reformation woodcuts, these old figures of public humiliation and social torture can be seen as early prototypes of modern blasphemous cartoons.

14. Shame mask.

It is striking how many punishments for blasphemy have
concentrated on the figure and the face. Being whipped through
the streets or standing in the pillory are as much about public
spectacles of defamation as physical torture. Branded with a big B
on his forehead, the Quaker James Nayler became a living
caricature. Defacing—in person and on paper—is an apposite

116

punishment for blasphemy, since one of the key meanings of blasphemy is damage to *fama*, fame/reputation. An eye for an eye. A face for a face.

Most blasphemy controversies about cartoons and pictures send a confusing double message: pictures are nothing, *and* pictures have extreme power, even power to cause pain. Those defending the Muhammad cartoon special issue in *Jyllands-Posten* often argued that damaging a picture of Muhammad caused no harm to the real Muhammad because these were only cartoons. But a journalist at *Jyllands-Posten* also described the cartoons as 'democratic electroshock therapy'. *Electroshock therapy* suggests that he imagined real hurt to the body of the community identifying with the Prophet. Electroshock therapy doesn't sound like something that someone would willingly sign up for—like hydrotherapy or a nice hot stone massage.

The *Charlie Hebdo* murders led to a deluge of cartoons about the power of pens and pencils in newspapers and on social media. Some presented pencils as the exact opposite of guns (Figure 15). Others presented pens and pencils as weapons that were bigger than guns: for example, a cartoon of a Rambo Charlie Hebdo, with massive weapon-pencils on his muscular arms (Figure 16).

15. Ixène, 'Asymmetrical War': pens versus weapons. One of the many cartoons responding to the *Charlie Hebdo* attacks in January 2015.

NOUS SOMMES TOUS CHARLIE HEBDO!...

ET NOUS NE DÉSARMERONS JAMAIS!

À WOLINSKI, CABU, CHARB... TIGNOUS...

KASH, KINSHASA, RDC 7.01.2014

16. 'We are all Charlie Hebdo, and we will never lay down our arms';
Kash, Kinshasa, Cartooning for Peace.

The pen/pencil is and is not like a gun. This conflict goes back to
the old adage (which can be tracked back at least as far as the
Bible): 'The word or pen is mightier (or sharper) than the sword.'
This statement can be read as 'The pen is mightier because the
pen is pacifist and *does not hurt*' or 'The pen is a *stronger* weapon,
with *greater power to hurt*.' Both conflicting ideas about the
powers of the pen have been regularly referenced in blasphemy
controversies. Penning a wordy riposte to the bishop who was so
determined to put him in jail, Thomas Woolston mocked: 'I shall
hide myself from the terrible strokes of [your] pen.' ('Sticks and
stones will break my bones but pens will never hurt me'. Or,
alternatively, 'You, Mr Bishop, have a teeny little pen.') The
Ahmadi Muslims who mounted a peaceful campaign against
David Low's accidental cartoon of Muhammad (Chapter 5)
described themselves as carrying out a pacifist *jihad* (meaning
'struggle'), not of the sword but 'of the pen'.

Screens and shop windows

Throughout this book we have discussed why blasphemy controversies and prosecutions did not decline in modernity, as is often imagined, but often intensified and increased. We have looked at some of the reasons for this, including new legislation (see Chapter 3) and the impact of religious pluralism (see Chapter 5). New media also contributed to the rise and intensification of blasphemy, by providing new platforms for disseminating and exhibiting blasphemies; recording hurt and creating communities of outrage; declaring sympathy and solidarity with 'blasphemies' and 'blasphemers'; tagging particular artworks and films with something like *#blasphemy*; assembling protesters by mobile phone apps; and making *news*. New media support new forms of blasphemy (such as Russian YouTuber Ruslan Sokolovskiy's film of himself playing Pokémon in church); new techniques for hiding the faces of 'blasphemers' (on one YouTube site, the poem 'The Love that Dares to Speak its Name' (Chapter 1) is read by a cartoon robot, so no one is responsible); and new forms of surveillance and censorship operated by institutions like the Indian Ministry of Communications and Information Technology, which, aided by algorithms and data collection, can really operate like an omniscient God.

Some media are, by their nature, far more vulnerable than others. To mark a unique *artwork* as 'blasphemous', all you need is an adept use of paint or hammers. Andreas Serrano's *Piss Christ* was attacked with hammers in Avignon on Palm Sunday. Chris Ofili's *The Holy Virgin Mary* was daubed with white paint. Galleries can remove or refuse to exhibit blasphemous artworks, even on the grounds that they *may* cause offence in the future (see the case of John Latham's *God is Great* in Chapter 3). Theatres can be picketed, as with the case of *Jerry Springer: The Opera*, or *Behzti* or the play *Golgota Picnic* in Toulouse and Paris, and 'blasphemous' plays and musicals can be forced from the stage.

Cinema is a highly regulated, and therefore particularly vulnerable, industry. Film classification boards can refuse a certificate. *Monty Python's Life of Brian* was never convicted of blasphemy in a court of law, but EMI films withdrew funding just days before production, and the film would never have been made had not George Harrison (of the Beatles) stepped in to finance the film at the last minute. Thirty-nine local authorities in the UK banned the film or imposed an X certificate (18 years), effectively preventing the film from being shown.

Refusing a certificate became a very effective para-legal method for enforcing 'blasphemy' charges in the case of Nigel Wingrove's film *Vision of Ecstasy* or Werner Schroeter's film *Liebeskonzil*. In France in the 1960s, Jacques Rivette's film *La Religieuse/The Nun* (based on the novel by Denis Diderot) was approved by the Censorship Board but blocked by the Minister of Information in response to a campaign by the Catholic Church. Rivette's film is one of the many 'blasphemies' that were never made.

If we take a sneak peak back at early religious cinema, the cliché that society has gradually become more permissive and open to blasphemy is undermined (once again). In *The Temptation of St Anthony* from 1898, St Anthony gets to see a fully naked woman. In Cecil B. DeMille's *The Sign of the Cross* (1932), the heroine, Claudette Colbert, takes a sexy milk bath and a naked female martyr appears (for unknown reasons) with a naughty gorilla (see Figure 17).

Such sexy-religious moments were soon stopped by *The Don'ts* and *Be Carefuls* and later the Motion Picture Production Codes of the late 1920s and early 1930s, established to clean up Hollywood's tawdry reputation. Concerned with precisely the same kinds of offences that had traditionally been packaged together in the idea of 'blasphemy', the new codes censured nudity and sex (including 'sex relationships between the white and black races'); ridicule of the clergy; bad use of words like 'God', 'Lord',

17. **Naked female martyr with a naughty gorilla in Cecil B. DeMille's**
The Sign of the Cross (1932).

'Jesus', 'Christ', 'hell', 'damn'; and also sedition and disrespectful
use of the flag.

It is an interesting exercise to go back over some of the
examples in this book and think about them again, this time
from the perspective of media. The surprisingly uncontroversial
monkey-eucharists or nuns picking phalluses from phallus trees

in the margins of medieval manuscripts (see Chapter 3) were one-offs, made by hand for one patron, which is why they passed without notice. Most representations of Muhammad's face and body come from illustrated manuscripts intended for elite, private audiences. In contrast, Reformation woodcuts of Protestants farting in the face of the Pope, or pope-donkeys, were part of a concerted print media campaign. The invention of the printing press and the age of mechanical reproduction changed the target of blasphemy prosecutions. Most 18th- and 19th-century 'blasphemies' were print blasphemies: cheap pamphlets, books, and (especially) newspapers, such as Abner Kneeland's *Boston Inquirer*, or George Foote's *The Freethinker*, or John Gott's *Truthseeker*, controversial because they were published at what Foote called the 'people's price'. We can assume that if blasphemers like Richard Carlile, William Hone, or Abner Kneeland had been alive in the age of the internet, they would have used it to good effect!

In the age before screens, many activist blasphemers used the 18th- and 19th-century equivalent: shop windows. Richard Carlile displayed 'blasphemous' effigies, which drew large crowds, in the window of his London Fleet Street shop, including effigies of a bishop and a devil arm in arm. Edinburgh bookseller Thomas Paterson was convicted in 1844 for displaying blasphemous placards in the window of his print shop. The last convicted blasphemer in the USA (convicted in 1928) was the atheist activist Charles Lee Smith, who rented a store in Little Rock, Arkansas and put a placard in the window reading 'Evolution Is True. The Bible's a Lie. God's a Ghost.' (Since, as an atheist, Lee could not take the religious oath required by the court, he was not permitted to testify in his own defence.) In 1971, two Pennsylvania booksellers faced prosecution for blasphemy for displaying, on a sign in their shop window, an old political Wanted poster from 1917: 'Jesus Christ—Wanted for sedition, criminal anarchy, vagrancy, and conspiracy to overthrow the established government...associates with common working people, unemployed, and bums. Alien, said to be a Jew.'

Transmitting blasphemy

The media revolutions from the 1880's onwards have greatly expanded capacities for making, amplifying, spreading, monitoring, and prosecuting 'blasphemies'. News of David Low's Muhammad cartoon in 1925 (see Chapter 5) was transmitted by telegraph to India. The fatwa against Rushdie was announced on Iranian radio, then faxed or telexed to the UK by the British embassy in Iran, just in time for a shocked Salman Rushdie to respond on the BBC lunchtime news. The loudspeakers of the local mosque and an interview with a local police officer on CNN were used to spread reports of Asia Bibi's 'blasphemies' in Pakistan. When the French art director Joachim Roncin tweeted the famous hashtag #*Je suis Charlie* it became the most retweeted meme in Twitter history. In a BBC interview in 2016, Roncin suggested that the meme became so popular because 'we were trying to feel a sense of community'.

It is not true, however, that new media like television or the internet allow blasphemies to be transmitted automatically, in a nanosecond, at the push of a button or a click of a mouse. British Muslims who felt insulted by *The Satanic Verses* tried to register the offence in the law courts, but this was impossible, since the only 'blasphemies' that had any legal existence were blasphemies against Anglican Christianity. They also failed, initially, in attempts to get public recognition through the *news*. On 2 December 1988, a small group of Muslims burnt a copy of the book in the British town of Bolton. There was no news coverage, and no one noticed. On 14 January 1989, they attempted a similar public display after informing the national media. Footage of the book-burning shows the journalist, who needs to get a photograph and copy in by 2 p.m., asking, 'Can you burn it earlier?' The book-burners oblige. This second time, the book-burning was videoed and dispatched to media outlets. As Kenan Malik comments, the British Muslim community learnt to appreciate 'the teaching of Marshall McLuhan (the famous media theorist) as well as the teaching of the prophet Muhammad'.

The Danish Cartoon Affair started as a local dispute between the low-circulation Aarhus newspaper *Jyllands-Posten* and local Muslim clerics. The graphic novelist Art Spiegelman hits on the right metaphor for the growth of the 'affair' when he says that the local cartoons '*metastasized* into a frenzy of international protests' (my emphasis). Metastasis tends to be slow. The cartoons were published on 30 September 2005. By February 2006, as a result of concerted media work, the cartoons had been reprinted in 143 newspapers in 56 countries and had been widely publicized through satellite television, online blogs, and bulletin boards in mosques. European and Scandinavian newspapers, including *Charlie Hebdo*, published the cartoons, while North American and British news outlets tended either not to publish, or to only show 'responsible glimpses' or pixillated pictures.

The fires of the 'affair' were stoked by a doctored dossier taken by Danish imams to Egypt, which added three scandalous images to the twelve cartoons. These were a crudely photoshopped picture of a dog on the back of a praying Muslim; a crudely drawn image of the prophet holding two tiny women, like puppets, one in each hand, with the caption 'The paedophile prophet'; and a blurry photograph of a man wearing pig ears and a snout later identified as a picture of a contestant in a French pig-squealing contest but presented, in the dossier, with the caption: 'This is a true picture of Muhammad'. Ironically, even as the BBC tried to balance freedom of expression against religious sensitivity by showing the images in 'responsible glimpses', they also showed the pig-snout picture in the batch of offending cartoons.

The affair was fuelled by the journalistic principle of 'If it screams, or bleeds, it leads.' News outlets paid little attention to rallies and peaceful demonstrations, or the letter from the government of Egypt to the Danish Prime Minister stating that 'Your excellency rightly underlined that terrorists should not be allowed to abuse Islam for their crimes. In the same token, Danish press and public representatives should not be allowed to abuse Islam in the name of democracy, freedom of expression, and human rights, values that we all share.' But they started to tune into, and help to make, the affair, when the Iranian president, Mahmoud Ahmadinejad, decided to escalate the cartoon affair into a cartoons 'arms race' by opening a competition for cartoons mocking the holocaust, and when protesters started to burn flags, those sacred pieces of cloth symbolizing the nation-state. Danish flags and American flags were targeted. Despite the fact that North American news outlets had tended not to show the cartoons, the American flag was seen as the holy icon of the blasphemous West. Mass demonstrations over the cartoons were among the first demonstrations organized by mobile phone. In Lahore, Beirut, and Damascus they left 248 people dead.

The 'affair' only erupted five months after the cartoons were first published. One of the vigilante acts of retribution was a very contemporary form of media protest: a cyberattack. Justifying his attack on Danish websites in February 2006, the Hacker Darkblood wrote: 'On Sept 29th, 2005 issue of *Jyllands-Posten*, I saw and read dreadful news and cartoons.' But the cartoons were published on 30 September. Darkblood had looked them up online, where the posting date was a day earlier. Like Lord Chief Justice Hamilton, inviting the jury to reimagine their first shock encounter with James Kirkup's poem (see Chapter 4), Darkblood was imagining the first shock encounter with the cartoons.

Jytte Klausen observes: 'The cartoons took on a life of their own. They became avatars.' *Avatar* is a perfect word. Derived from the Sanskrit word for a god or soul in bodily form, an avatar is an online persona embodying the community or individual it represents. The Muhammad cartoons became avatars for the Muslim community; for pro-blasphemy communities arguing for freedom of expression; and also for the media. As Klausen sagely comments: 'Stories generated stories as the global media started to cover *itself*.'

Blasphemy and blasphemy-by-algorithm

In the late 19th century, George Foote and Léo Taxil could count on readers who still knew the Bible and Christian tradition in intimate detail. In Taxil's Bible, no less than 401 cartoons riff on now obscure Bible stories (including even Naboth's vineyard, discussed in Chapter 2). In contrast, contemporary blasphemies tend to take the form of easily recognizable signs, repeated over and over again: Muhammad cartoons; burnt and defaced Qur'ans; gay or trans religious figures; and animals on the cross. These easily recognisable blasphemy memes reflect a decline of literacy in the Christian tradition, but also an expansion of blasphemy to include attacks on other religions about which relatively little is known, leading to repetitions around the few signs that are recognizable to outsiders. But they have also been generated by the so-called '8 second attention span' and the speeding up of modern information technology, creating blasphemies that can be read in an instant, like a catchy twitterfeed or the logo of a well known brand.

Whether they have been convicted by law, public protest or the actions taken by theatre and museum committees, many 'blasphemers' protest that their work has been reduced to reductive memes or completely obscured by media sensationalization. Comedian Stewart Lee is bemused as to why the alleged blasphemy of his musical *Jerry Springer: The Opera* was reduced to the one-line tag line 'gay Jesus wears a nappy', which was then repeated across media outlets, since Jesus never wears a nappy in the musical. Martin Kippenberger's frog on the cross only became blasphemous when a politician, Franz Pahl, performed his outrage by going on hunger strike (see Chapter 1). At first (before she lost the battle and was fired) the director of the Museion art museum in Bolzano, Italy responded by keeping Kippenberger's controversial amphibian on show, but now veiled by newspaper cuttings from the world press: a clear protest that the media event of 'blasphemy' had completely obscured the exhibition.

Blasphemy has also become an explicit form of *advertising and promotion*. It is nothing new to use a little bit of blasphemy to help circulation. The old biblical prophets used offence to get the attention of their audiences, for example by making shocking word-caricatures of drunken priests, or addressing their (male) audiences as prostitutes or she-asses on heat. Foote's *Freethinker* and Gott's *Truthseeker* both used the headline PROSECUTED FOR BLASPHEMY to add a soupçon of sensationalism and help boost sales. But blasphemers like Gott and Foote were campaigning for major causes such as the right to be secular, or what Gott called 'mental freedom and social progress'. They were the kind of blasphemers who deliberately vandalized the old holy things to add weight and sanctity to new sacred values, such as universal suffrage, anti-war protest, or birth control.

In contrast, in what I think of as a culture of *hashtag blasphemy*, blasphemy becomes a logo to create celebrity and keep flagging celebrity alive. When singer Nikki Minaj posed in a bikini in front of a statue of the Buddha (deliberately repeating offences that unwitting tourists had committed by accident by wearing bikinis or photographing themselves kissing the Buddha at sacred sites in Sri Lanka), she was not asserting her secular right to mock the Buddha, nor was she trying to give Buddhists some 'democratic electroshock therapy' by encouraging them to take the criticism of their sacred figures on the chin. Nor was she engaging in a protest against the repression of female sexuality by patriarchal religions, like the Femen activist Inna Shevchenko, who felled a large cross in Kiev with a chainsaw in an action that led to death threats and the activist seeking asylum in France. Instead, Nikki Menaj was simply trying, in a saturated mediasphere, to create 'click-bait' and 'likes'. The same could be said of Benetton's controversial poster campaign of a pope kissing an imam in 2011. In 2019, the Spanish studio The Game Kitchen launched a new video game called *Blasphemous*, using the gaming aesthetic of Catholic gothic. The word 'blasphemy' might not have a great deal of meaning or precision, but at the level of affect and emotion, this salacious word sells.

These new blasphemies are a very long way from George Grosz's *Christ in a Gas Mask*, or Pasolini's *La Ricotta*, or Ashraf Fayadh's poetry. They seem to fulfil G. K. Chesterton and T. S. Eliot's dark prophecies about the new god of economy and 'economic determinism' replacing 'philosophical conviction' (see Chapter 2). Blasphemy can now refer to the most minor acts of celebrity—as well as to brave campaigns for the right to freedom of expression and religious freedom. It can refer to absolute trivia, but it can also point to 'big visions' and 'cries for the moon'.

To end on a dystopian note, we are now entering a unique phase in history where 'blasphemies' and insults are being autogenerated by machines. Online gamers, influencers, and 'trolls' like Felix Arvid Ulf Kjelberg (better known to his 100 million subscribers as Pewdie Pie), deliberately use offensive and taboo subjects to maximize their followers, and therefore their revenue. Optimized for viewer engagement, the algorithms used by Google and Facebook are programmed to fuel conflict, because studies have shown that controversy keeps viewers engaged for far longer than constructive debate. Algorithms contributed to the shocking backlash against social justice movements like #MeToo or Black Lives Matter, because they were programmed to disseminate campaign statements not to those who would *like* them, but to those who would be most likely not to like them, indeed to be incited by them—and therefore spend a longer time (as we euphemistically say) engaged. Today, blasphemy is not being killed off by 'economic determinism', as T. S. Eliot and G. K. Chesterton feared. Instead, economic determinism is now producing 'blasphemies'.

Now, more than ever, we need a nuanced rather than a one-size-fits-all approach to blasphemy—because a 'blasphemer' is just as likely to be an algorithm in an unregulated internet as a life-risking campaigner for freedom of religion and freedom of speech.

References and further reading

Chapter 1: Introduction: 'blasphemous' crucifixions

Julie Clague, 'The Christa: Symbolising my Humanity and my Pain', *Feminist Theology* 1 (2005)

Christiane Kruse, Birgit Meyer, and Anne-Marie Korte, *Taking Offence: Religion, Art and Visual Culture in Plural Configurations* (Paderborn, 2013)

David Lawton, *Blasphemy* (Philadelphia, 1993)

Leonard Levy, *Blasphemy: Verbal Offense against the Sacred from Moses to Salman Rushdie* (Chapel Hill, NC, 1995)

David Nash, *Blasphemy in Modern Britain: 1789 to the Present* (London, 1999)

Pier Paolo Pasolini, *La Ricotta* ('Curd Cheese'), part of the omnibus film Ro.Go.Pa.G; available as the supplement to *Mama Roma* (Criterion, 1962)

Charles Taylor, *Sources of the Self: The Making of the Modern Identity* (Cambridge, Mass., 1989)

Joan E. Taylor (ed.), *Jesus and Brian: Exploring the Historical Jesus and his Times via Monty Python's Life of Brian* (London, 2015)

Chapter 2: Blasphemy in scarequotes

Talal Asad, Wendy Brown, Judith Butler, and Saba Mahmood, *Is Critique Secular? Blasphemy, Injury and Free Speech* (Berkeley, 2009)

Timothy Beal, 'Pussy Riot's Theology', *The Chronicle of Higher Education*, September 17, 2012

Anya Bernstein, 'An Inadvertent Sacrifice: Body Politics and Sovereign Power in the Pussy Riot Affair', *Critical Inquiry* 40.1 (2013)

Asia Bibi and Anne-Isabelle Tollet, *Blasphemy, a Memoir: Sentenced to Death over a Cup of Water* (Chicago, 2013)

Alain Cabantous, *Blasphemy: Impious Speech in the West from the Seventeenth to the Nineteenth Century* (New York, 2002)

Charb, *Open Letter: On Blasphemy, Islamophobia and the True Enemies of Free Expression* (New York, 2016)

G. K. Chesterton, *Heretics* (London, 1905)

Régis Debray and Didier Leschi, *La Laïcité au quotidien* (Paris, 2016) (=*Everyday Secularism: A Practical Guide*)

T. S. Eliot, *After Strange Gods: A Primer on Modern Heresy* (London, 1934)

Ashraf Fayadh, *Instructions Within* (New York, 2016)

Paul Finckelman, 'Blasphemy and Free Thought in Jacksonian America: The Case of Abner Kneeland', in Grenda et al. (eds), *Profane*

Michel Foucault, *Fearless Speech* (London, 2001)

Masha Geshen, *Words will Break Cement: The Passion of Pussy Riot* (London, 2014)

Christopher Grenda, Chris Beneke, and David Nash (eds), *Profane: Sacrilegious Expression in a Multicultural Age* (Oakland, Calif., 2014)

F. LaGard Smith, *Blasphemy and the Battle for Faith* (London, 1990) (LaGard Smith is the author who describes blasphemy as the 'feeling that one gets when his house is broken into…' etc.)

Stewart Lee, *Don't Get me Started: What's Wrong with Blasphemy?* <https://www.youtube.com/watch?v=N9EUe8jNr6o>

David Nash, *Blasphemy in the Christian World: A History* (Oxford, 2010)

Pussy Riot: A Punk Prayer (BBC Storyville, 21 October 2013)

Yvonne Sherwood, *Biblical Blaspheming: Trials of the Sacred for a Secular Age* (Cambridge, 2012)

David Tollerton, *Holocaust Memory and Britain's Religious-Secular Landscape* (London, 2020)

Robert Yelle, 'Secular Blasphemies: Symbolic Offences in Modern Democracy', in Grenda et al. (eds), *Profane*

Chapter 3: Blasphemy and religion

Janaka Ashin and Kate Crosby, 'Heresy and Monastic Malpractice in the Buddhist Court Cases (*Vinicchaya*) of Modern Bhurma (Myanmar)', *Contemporary Buddhism* 18 (2017)

Michael Camille, *Image on the Edge: The Margins of Medieval Art* (London, 2019)

Wendy Doniger, *The Hindus: An Alternative History* (London, 2009)

Wendy Doniger, 'Prelude to Censorship: The Toleration of Blasphemy in Ancient India', *Sightings*, 21 May 2015 <https://divinity. uchicago.edu/sightings/articles/prelude-censorship-toleration-blasphemy-ancient-india>

Christiane Gruber, *The Praiseworthy One: The Prophet Muhammad in Islamic Texts and Images* (Bloomington, Ind., 2019)

Thomas Hoffmann and J. Christiansen, 'Paradoxes, Loopholes, and Invitations in Qur'ānic Polemic', in Mehdi Azaiez and Mokdad Arfa Menzia (eds), *Contextualizing and Interpreting the Qur'ān* (Bristol, 2021)

Raminder Kaur and William Mazzarella (eds), *Censorship in South Asia: Cultural Regulation from Sedition to Seduction* (Bloomington, Ind., 2009)

Ze'ev Maghen, 'The Merry Men of Medina: Comedy and Humanity in the Early Days of Islam', *Der Islam* 83 (2008)

Elham Manea, 'In the Name of Culture and Religion: The Political Function of Blasphemy in Islamic States', *Islam and Christian–Muslim Relations* 27.1 (2016)

Joss Marsh, *Word Crimes: Blasphemy, Culture and Literature in Nineteenth Century England* (Chicago, 1998)

Tomoko Masuzawa, *The Invention of World Religions, or How European Universalism was Preserved in the Language of Pluralism* (Chicago, 2005)

Ebrahim Moosa, 'Muslim Political Theology: Defamation, Apostasy and Anathema', in Grenda et al. (eds), *Profane*

Intisar A. Rabb, 'Society and Propriety: The Cultural Construction of Defamation and Blasphemy as Crimes in Islamic Law', in Camilla Adang, Hassan Ansari, Maribel Fierro, and Sabine Schmidtke (eds), *Accusations of Unbelief in Islam: A Diachronic Perspective on Takfīr* (Leiden, 2015)

Paul Rollier, Kathinka Frøystad, and Arild Engelsen Ruud (eds), *Outrage: The Rise of Religious Offence in Contemporary South Asia* (London, 2019)

Abdullah Saeed, 'Ambiguities of Apostasy and the Repression of Muslim Dissent', *Review of Faith and International Affairs* 9.2 (2011)

Yvonne Sherwood, 'Binding-Unbinding: Pre-critical "Critique" in Pre-modern Jewish, Christian and Islamic Responses to the Sacrifice of Abraham/Ibrahim's Son', in Sherwood, *Biblical Blaspheming*

Terje Stordalen and Birgit Meyer (eds), *Figurations and Sensations of the Unseen in Judaism, Christianity and Islam* (London, 2019)

Chapter 4: Blasphemy and law

The European Legal Framework on Hate Speech, Blasphemy and its Interaction with Freedom of Expression 30.9 (2015) <http://www.europarl.europa.eu/RegData/etudes/STUD/2015/536460/IPOL_STU%282015%29536460_EN.pdf>

Bhairav Achraya, 'Free Speech in India: Still Plagued by Pre-modern Laws', *Media Asia* 42.3–4 (2015)

Heiner Bielefeldt, *Report of the Special Rapporteur on Freedom of Religion or Belief, UN General Assembly Religion and Violence* (29.12.2014) <www.ohchr.org/EN/HRBodies/HRC/.../A_HRC_28_66_ENG.doc>

Hypatia Bradlaugh-Bonner, *Penalties upon Opinion, or Some Records of the Laws of Heresy and Blasphemy* (London, 1934)

Shemeem Burney Abbas, *Pakistan's Blasphemy Law: From Islamic Empires to Taliban* (Austin, Tex., 2013)

Austin Dacey, *The Future of Blasphemy: Speaking of the Sacred in an Age of Human Rights* (London, 2012)

Joelle Fiss and Jocelyn Getgen Kestenbaun, *Respecting Rights: Measuring the World's Blasphemy Laws* (USCIRF=US Commission on International Religious Freedom, 2017)

Ian Leigh, 'Damned if They Do, Damned if They Don't: The European Court of Human Rights and the Protection of Religion from Attack', *Res Publica* 17 (2011)

Andreas Philippopoulos-Mihalopoulos, 'Atmospheres of Law: Senses, Affects, Lawscapes', *Emotion, Space and Society* 2.6 (2013)

Akhtar Rasool Bodla, 'Genesis of Blasphemy Laws in Colonial India', *Pakistan Journal of History and Culture* 38.2 (2017)

András Sajó (ed.), *Censorial Sensitivities: Free Speech and Religion in a Fundamentalist World* (Utrecht, 2007)

Catherine Schuler, 'Reinventing the Show Trial: Putin and Pussy Riot', *The Drama Review* 57.1 (2013)

Stephen Shapin, *The Social History of Truth: Civility and Science in Seventeenth-Century England* (Chicago, 2005)

Jeroen Temperman and András Koltay (eds), *Blasphemy and Freedom of Expression: Comparative, Theoretical and Historical Reflections after the Charlie Hebdo Massacre* (Cambridge, 2017)

Chapter 5: Blasphemy and minorities

Shabab Ahmed, *Before Orthodoxy: The Satanic Verses in Early Islam* (Cambridge, Mass., 2017)

M. M. Ahsan and A. R. Kidawi, *Sacrilege versus Civility: Muslim Perspectives on the Satanic Verses Affair* (Leicester, 1991)

James Bloodworth, 'Today Everyone wants to Defend Salman Rushdie: It Was not Always like That', *The Independent*, 24 September 2012

Geoffrey Brahm Levey and Tariq Modood, 'The Muhammad Cartoons and Multicultural Democracies', *Ethnicities* 9 (2009)

Jeanne Favret-Saada, 'An Anthropology of Religious Polemics: The Case of Blasphemy Affairs', *HAU* 6.1 (2016)

Gurpreet Kaur Bhatti, *Behzti* (London, 2004)

Ruqayya Yasmin Khan, *Muhammad in the Digital Age* (Austin, 2015)

Signe Engelbreth Larsen, 'Towards the Blasphemous Self: Constructing Societal Identity in Danish Debates on the Blasphemy Provision in the Twentieth and Twenty-First Centuries', *Journal of Ethnic and Migration Studies* 40.2 (2014)

David Low, *Low's Autobiography* (London, 1965)

Kenan Malik, *From Fatwa to Jihad: The Rushdie Affair and its Legacy* (London, 2009)

Salman Rushdie, 'The New Empire within Britain', in Rushdie, *Imaginary Homelands* (New York, 1982)

Salman Rushdie Fatwa, 30 Years On (BBC *Newsnight*, 11 February 2019)

The Satanic Verses Affair (BBC2, 7 March 2009)

Laura Schwartz, *Infidel Feminism: Secularism, Religion and Women's Emancipation, England, 1830–1914* (Manchester, 2013)

Yvonne Sherwood, 'The Old Threat of Secularism and the New Threat of Islam', *The Immanent Frame* 04/06/2015 <https://tif.ssrc.org/2015/04/06/blasphemous-cartoons-the-old-threat-of-secularism-and-the-new-threat-of-islam/>

Yvonne Sherwood, 'Christians, Jews, Muslims and Blasphemy ACH (After *Charlie Hebdo*) and BSV=Before *The Satanic Verses*', in Yolande Jansen and Nasar Meer (eds), *Patterns of Prejudice*, special issue Genealogies of 'Jews' and 'Muslims': Social Imaginaries in the Race–Religion Nexus April 2020 https://www.tandfonline.com/toc/rpop20/54/1–2?nav=tocList. A longer discussion of the David Low and George Foote cartoons can be found in this article.

Emmanuel Todd, *Who is Charlie? Xenophobia and the New Middle Class* (Cambridge, 2015)

Salil Tripathi, 'Women who Fought for Salman Rushdie', 21 February 2019 <https://www.livemint.com/news/india/women-who-fought-for-salman-rushdie-1550711196234.html>

Richard Webster, *A Brief History of Blasphemy: Liberalism, Censorship and The Satanic Verses* (Southwold, 1990)

Fay Weldon, *Sacred Cows: A Portrait of Britain, Post-Rushdie, Pre-Utopia* (London, 1989)

Chapter 6: Blasphemy and media

Algorithms Rule us All. VPRO Documentary, YouTube (27 October 2018)

Webb Keane, *Christian Moderns: Freedom and Fetish in the Mission Encounter* (Oakland, Calif., 2006)

W. J. T. Mitchell, *What do Pictures Want? The Lives and Loves of Images* (Chicago, 2005)

Brent Plate, *Blasphemy: Art that Offends* (London, 2006)

Art Spiegelman, 'Drawing Blood: Outrageous Cartoons and the Art of Outrage', *Harpers*, June 2006

Johanna Sumiala, '"Je suis Charlie" and the Digital Mediascape: The Politics of Death in the Charlie Hebdo Mourning Rituals', *Journal of Ethnology and Folkloristics* 11.1 (2017)

Sigrid Weigel, *Grammatologie der Bilder* (Berlin, 2015)

Index

For the benefit of digital users, indexed terms that span two pages (e.g., 52–53) may, on occasion, appear on only one of those pages.

Index

CATHOLICISM
A Very Short Introduction
Gerald O'Collins

Despite a long history of external threats and internal strife, the
Roman Catholic Church and the broader reality of Catholicism
remain a vast and valuable presence into the third millennium of
world history. What are the origins of the Catholic Church? How
has Catholicism changed and adapted to such vast and diverse
cultural influences over the centuries? What great challenges
does the Catholic Church now face in the twenty-first century,
both within its own life and in its relation to others around the
world? In this Very Short Introduction, Gerald O'Collins draws on
the best current scholarship available to answer these questions
and to present, in clear and accessible language, a fresh
introduction to the largest and oldest institution in the world.

www.oup.com/vsi

CHRISTIAN ETHICS
A Very Short Introduction
D. Stephen Long

This *Very Short Introduction* to Christian ethics introduces the topic by examining its sources and historical basis. D. Stephen Long presents a discussion of the relationship between Christian ethics, modern, and postmodern ethics, and explores practical issues including sex, money, and power. Long recognises the inherent difficulties in bringing together 'Christian' and 'ethics' but argues that this is an important task for both the Christian faith and for ethics. Arguing that Christian ethics are not a precise science, but the cultivation of practical wisdom from a range of sources, Long also discusses some of the failures of the Christian tradition, including the crusades, the conquest, slavery, inquisitions, and the Galileo affair.

www.oup.com/vsi

FREE SPEECH
A Very Short Introduction
Nigel Warburton

'I disapprove of what you say, but I will defend to the death your right to say it' This slogan, attributed to Voltaire, is frequently quoted by defenders of free speech. Yet it is rare to find anyone prepared to defend all expression in every circumstance, especially if the views expressed incite violence. So where do the limits lie? What is the real value of free speech? Here, Nigel Warburton offers a concise guide to important questions facing modern society about the value and limits of free speech: Where should a civilized society draw the line? Should we be free to offend other people's religion? Are there good grounds for censoring pornography? Has the Internet changed everything? This Very Short Introduction is a thought-provoking, accessible, and up-to-date examination of the liberal assumption that free speech is worth preserving at any cost.

'The genius of Nigel Warburton's *Free Speech* lies not only in its extraordinary clarity and incisiveness. Just as important is the way Warburton addresses freedom of speech - and attempts to stifle it - as an issue for the 21st century. More than ever, we need this book.'

Denis Dutton, University of Canterbury, New Zealand

www.oup.com/vsi

RELIGION IN AMERICA
A Very Short Introduction
Timothy Beal

Timothy Beal describes many aspects of religion in contemporary
America that are typically ignored in other books on the subject,
including religion in popular culture and counter-cultural groups;
the growing phenomenon of "hybrid" religious identities, both
individual and collective; the expanding numbers of new religious
movements, or NRMs, in America; and interesting examples
of "outsider religion." He also offers an engaging overview of the
history of religion in America, from Native American traditions to
the present day. Finally, Beal highlights the three major forces
shaping the present and future of religion in America.

THE REFORMATION
A Very Short Introduction
Peter Marshall

The Reformation transformed Europe, and left an indelible mark on the modern world. It began as an argument about what Christians needed to do to be saved, but rapidly engulfed society in a series of fundamental changes. This *Very Short Introduction* provides a lively and up-to-date guide to the process. Peter Marshall argues that the Reformation was not a solely European phenomenon, but that varieties of faith exported from Europe transformed Christianity into a truly world religion. It explains doctrinal debates in a clear and non-technical way, but is equally concerned to demonstrate the effects the Reformation had on politics, society, art, and minorities.